Home Office Know-How

Jeffery D. Zbar

Upstart
Publishing Company®
Specializing in Small Business Publishing
a division of Dearborn Publishing Group, Inc.

This publication is designed to provide accurate and authoritative information in regard to the subject matter covered. It is sold with the understanding that neither the publisher nor the author is engaged in rendering legal, accounting, or other professional service. If legal advice or other expert assistance is required, the services of a competent professional person should be sought.

Acquisitions Editor: Danielle Egan-Miller
Managing Editor: Jack Kiburz
Interior Design: Elizandro Carrington
Cover Design: Design Alliance, Inc.
Typesetting: Elizabeth Pitts

Published by Upstart Publishing Company,® a division of Dearborn Publishing Group, Inc.

Printed in the United States of America

98 99 00 10 9 8 7 6 5 4 3 2 1

Library of Congress Cataloging-in-Publication Data

Zbar, Jeffery D.
    Home office know-how / by Jeffery D. Zbar.
      p. cm.
    ISBN 1-57410-104-8 (pbk.)
     1. Home-based businesses—Management.   2. New business
enterprises. I. Title.
HD62.38.Z33 1998
658'.041—dc21
                                  98-20981
                                    CIP

Contents

Preface

It was a defining moment in the career of this work-at-home dad. Miss Shiela, my daughter Nicole's preschool teacher, had asked what work each pupil's parents do.

Innocent enough question, and the four-year-olds' answers came forth with a preschooler's simplicity. Some daddies were doctors, some mommies were lawyers. Some were real estate agents, some worked in offices, and some stayed at home.

Then there was Nicole. "My mommy is a nurse," said Nicole, "and my daddy goes to work in his underwear."

Truth be told, yes, I do occasionally work in my underwear. When it's 5 AM and I've just crawled out of bed, the house is quiet and dark, and the sun has yet to rise over the Atlantic, I could well be in my skivvies. Trust me, it's not as cute a picture as the work-at-home mom in bunny slippers in television commercials. But as a work-at-home parent, this attire is entirely acceptable.

After Nicole's unwitting acknowledgment, the grapevine grew ripe. Miss Shiela knowingly smiled. Nicole's classmates chuckled. Then all proceeded to tell their parents, who then wondered aloud to my wife, Robbie. She just nodded. We were either admired by those who wish they—or their spouse—could make a living working from home. Or we were admonished by traditionalists for not getting "a real job."

Since the day in February 1989 when I walked out of an ill-paying day job to make my break as a home-based freelance writer, I've been defining and redefining my work and rediscovering my relationship with my family and myself.

Today, we're raising three children. There are no day-care services to bleed us dry or nannies who are unimpressed by the giddy baby steps of childhood development. It's just Robbie and me, and a strong support system of family and friends, all working together to make this work style work.

Who knew in 1989, when we launched my enterprise, that I would be the "bleeding edge" of a work style trend that—along with its close cousin teleworking—would shake up the cubicle-lined structure of the nation's workplace. Every day, people are quitting a day job to go solo at home or are working up the nerve to ask their boss or manager about teleworking arrangements that would have them splitting their workweek between a traditional and a home office. Today, the numbers approach 50 million people working from home full-time or part-time for themselves or their boss back at the corporate office.

My first year—11 months in all—I billed $6,000. I was elated with my apparent success. My wife and in-laws were not amused. But with Robbie's income and, more important, her emotional support, I built a successful business that eventually allowed her to work part-time. All this while suffering the single telephone line, slow-paying clients, and power interruptions that erased from memory hours of work (this was before inexpensive uninterrupted power supplies, and before I had sense enough to save my work on a regular basis).

Today, the business has evolved. Those who have worked from home beyond the two-year honeymoon period know the trials the setting presents. How do you gently steer those clients who don't know their vendor works from home—but want to hold a meeting at *your* office—to an off-site location? How do you muffle the daily sounds of household life? How do you gain acceptance from family and friends? How do you take your business to the next level?

These questions once confronted me daily. But with a steady steam of loyal clients, I don't worry the day-to-day. And I get to surround myself with what is important: going to my kids' school functions and volunteering in their classrooms, breaking on a Tuesday afternoon for a quick swim, or listening as our infant coos on the office floor behind me as I work. All this while I continue to build a successful at-home business.

Today's emerging solo flyer will walk a path pioneered by others. Where we suffered from executives who wouldn't take seriously a work-at-home professional, today we're part of the working landscape. Even friends and family now know that this is not "that little thing I do from home." This is serious business, no different than if I got into a car at seven every morning and commuted with my fellow drones to the corporate hive downtown.

Actually, it is different. Very different. And very cool.

You ought to try it some time.

Acknowledgments

Working from home is nothing if not a collaborative effort between the solo flyer and the support crew. Workers, their family or friends, and the professional contacts they interact with daily, can all serve to promote or stifle the work-at-home process, its acceptance, and its ultimate failure—or success.

That said, I would like to thank my wife, Robbie, and children, Nicole, Zachary, and Zoe, each of whom has helped make my endeavors professionally successful and personally rewarding. Their involvement has helped me hone my understanding of this work-at-home work style, and their tolerance of this setup has allowed me to make a living from an erstwhile bedroom.

Thanks also go to my editors, editorial contacts, and sources, all of whom have had a hand in my ability to prosper. My editors have accepted my work arrangement, and my sources have tolerated interviews occasionally conducted above the din of household life. Their openmindedness is appreciated.

Certainly with three kids scampering about, working from home can border on mayhem at times. But there's nothing like watching your children grow under your own watchful and awed gaze. Short of coming up with this week's winning Lotto numbers, if I must work, this, my friends, is where I belong.

Introduction

So you're committed.

You've bought the furniture and the computer hardware. The business telephone line has been installed, and the fax/data line is plugged into the back of your computer. You're hot-wired to the world and ready to become a self-employed entrepreneur, a solo flyer.

Or maybe all that was done years ago. You may be a veteran at this work-at-home gig. But the octane seems to be waning, and the billings or the functionality of the at-home business seem flat.

There's more to running a successful home-based business than hooking up the hardware and telephone lines and hanging out a shingle. Those who have found success working from home know it takes more than the headstrong and impassioned fortitude of the modern, agile entrepreneur. It also takes marketing savvy, a basic knowledge of accounting principles, and acceptance from family and friends. It is a collaborative effort from a broad supporting cast.

This is the 1990's version of the American Dream: People launching their own enterprise from home and making a living at it. Statistics say almost 50 million people do some work from home. Whether they're running a business from home, teleworking from a day job, or bringing work home from the traditional office, working from a home office requires discipline, understanding. But working in that cocoon, it's difficult to learn what works best.

A few weeks into this journey and "committed" takes on a whole new meaning. All that time you spent calculating your savings, finding a work space, and deciding you can make this thing called "home-based entrepreneurship" work will be for naught if the panic and paranoia of actually being alone in the business world come calling. Checks will come slowly at times. At other times, receivables will come pouring in, making you flush with income and giddy with apparent success.

What about when the honeymoon's over, and the initial glee has subsided? Many who study and consult on the work-at-home phenomenon claim that the initial elation of working on one's own subsides after around 18 months. The charm has dulled, and the problems of entrepreneurship and self-employment begin to mount. Many decide this is the time to pull out of the race.

Instead, they should shift into second gear, hit the accelerator, and shoot for the checkered flag.

Working from home is a mind game. If you're motivated, then you're a workaholic. You family gets irked when you put in long hours—or work through dinner. And your friends don't understand why you won't break at noon on a Friday to clown around. Meanwhile, you're slaving to meet a deadline, wondering if that promised check will arrive in time to pay some bills—all while you scout for new business.

Are you really ready for the long-term commitment? Sure, entrepreneurship is what America was built on, and building a new business and being your own boss is integral to the American Dream. Your seemingly free schedule and time spent at home instead of commuting will make you the envy of your friends.

But there's a lot of work that goes into building a successful home-based business. Consider the downside: isolation, solitude, removal from the corporate culture, socking away cash to meet quarterly tax payments, friends and family who refuse to "get it" and insist on dropping by or calling on you midway during the daily grind.

Alas, there's a silver lining to all this. You become your own boss, set your own hours, hang with the family, keep an eye on the neighborhood, watch your kids grow up. This ain't the "Ozzie-and-Harriet" model. It's something your parents likely never had.

Still keen on pushing this working from home thing? If so, then read on.

Taking the Plunge
12 Tips to Hitting the Ground Running

Whether you already work from home or are planning to make a break for the greener pastures of at-home self-employment, how you make that initial leap is essential to your success. As carpenters say, measure twice, cut once. *Plan, plan, plan.* Everything from the office to the furniture and hardware to the profession you'll ply. Put in some serious brain time before hanging that shingle.

1. Get psyched. At the beginning of a home-based business venture, it's easy to get dogged by perplexing questions like what if . . . and am I nuts? Instead, many solo flyers forget the questions of sanity and focus on "what if" from a positive perspective. What if I succeed, outpace projections, need to move into a larger space? This was a promotion from employee to entrepreneur, and entrepreneurs are positive thinkers. Once the honeymoon is over, take it to the next level. A mantra to live by: B-E A-G-G-R-E-S-S-I-V-E! Passivity is OK if you're Swiss and there's a war. But not in business. Be competitive, agile, sharp, and unswayed by the initial slights and jabs that might come from peers, family, and friends. They're just jealous and don't understand the plan. Once you're successful, they'll get the picture—and admire you for it.

2. Choose wisely. What job works best from home—for the long haul? For many who already work from home, moving from corporate drone to self-employed was a matter of taking existing skills from one workplace to another. For others, it was a clean break and a chance to launch a new career. Choose wisely. Investigate growth industries, especially in your community or region. Take your knowledge base and use it in your new venture so you're not daunted by the learning curve.

3. Plan ahead. Will the home office you create today—from its placement in your home to the furniture and computer you buy—serve your needs tomorrow? Home offices don't relocate easily, and furniture isn't cheap. Envision where you think you'll be in a few years and you'll have fewer surprises down the road.

4. Look sharp. Create attractive stationery—especially business cards and Rolodex cards with your name or subject on the tab. And spread them freely! Marketing will be essential to your new venture, and your stationery is your calling card. You'll need to learn how to sell yourself and your product aggressively and inexpensively. So read, learn, and absorb from every available source.

5. Save something for Uncle Sam. Many are the home-based businesses that fall behind in quarterly tax payments. Not only is it your responsibility to pay up, but not doing so will place the weight of a serious albatross on your shoulders. Make it easy on yourself; set funds aside every month to meet those payments.

6. Ease on in. Removal from the corporate hive takes a transition. If the home office stint is to follow a full-time position, establish an office before you head out on your own. Get comfortable in the home office environs. Spend some time there. Settle in, if only to do some reading or get your papers and files in order. This will help you get acquainted with the space, learn where things work best, and diminish the culture shock when you move in for good.

7. Call all acquaintances. If word of mouth is the best form of advertising, then get talking. Spin the Rolodex, cruise through the contact manager software, open the little black book. Let people know you're on your own. Before you quit, tell confidants you'll be making the move; after you've quit, tell the world. Call friends from the old job and anyone in a related field and let them know you're flying solo. Schedule meetings with potential clients, customers, and others who can steer business your way. That will help keep you motivated and give you something to while away the initial slow transition period as you seek out work from potential clients.

8. Burn no bridges. Leave the corporate setting on good terms because yesterday's boss might be tomorrow's client. Tell your former manager that you'd be willing to take on some assignments for the company or keep doing the same work while the company looks for your replacement. In some instances, this can be the first contract the new business signs—and if handled well, it could last for a time, providing a cushion while you land other accounts.

9. Lay down the law. Possibly the hardest facet of working from home is getting the family and friends to understand that this isn't "that little thing you do from home." This new venture ultimately will put bread on the family table, clothes on the kids' backs, and cash in the pocket for life's little extras. Indoctrinate family and friends about the rules of this new work arrangement—when the office is off limits, when not to bug daddy or mommy, when not to call for some impromptu afternoon plans. Become a flexible enforcer who's willing to cut loose when the schedule's light and you could use a break.

10. Don't ignore the law. Learn about local laws and zoning regulations and how they affect a home-based business because ignorance of the law is no excuse. Many cities restrict or ban home-based businesses, signage, client visits, or on-site, nonresident employees. Learn what's allowed in your municipality, then make your decision. Many home-based workers are "guerrilla" entrepreneurs, working without permits and hiding in the shadows for fear that their city will deny their application or shut them down. Don't lurk in guilt; lobby for change.

11. Become a small office/home office (SOHO) evangelist. Many in the corporate community still are inexperienced and downright resentful when it comes to the small office/home office trend. Help introduce them to the benefits of working with those who work from home. Tell them of the cost savings they'll experience from your decreased overhead (no more real estate and desk space, benefits, taxes, and other incidentals). Convince them that you—and those like you—are more productive because you're more satisfied and can be depended upon to complete projects.

12. Enjoy the ride. The whole idea behind working from home in the first place is being your own boss, setting your own rules—and having the power to bend them when the spirit moves you. Is the hometown team playing this afternoon? If you can afford the time, take in a game at the ballpark. The youngster has a recital? What's more important in the grand scheme of things? After all, you can always burn some midnight oil to meet that deadline. Your child won't remember the time you spent on the phone or computer. But as the kids grow older, they will come to appreciate the quality hours you spent with them. This ride called life only comes around once. Enjoy the ride.

LOG ON AND LEARN

Visit these Web sites to learn more from fellow solo flyers. Get on a search engine (see the chapter titled "Tools"), plug in "home office," and seek out some sites of your own. Most have links to other pertinent SOHO sites. Build a list of your favorites, and visit them frequently to learn more.

www.aahbb.org

The site of the American Association of Home Based Businesses. This site provides content on the organization's information and lobbying efforts, as well as links to top work-at-home sites and content providers.

www.gohome.com

This site is the online version of *Business@Home* magazine, the former quarterly publication, and is also known as The Home Office Hub. It offers tips on marketing, business profiles from around the country, and the "Back Porch" light or poignant feature.

www.homebiznetwork.net

This site of Canadian home office radio host Allan Holander includes info on his "Home Biz Show" as well as various books, tapes, and marketing tips.

www.homebusiness.com

This is the site of the American Home Business Association (AHBA) of Salt Lake City, Utah, and is a complementary media outlet to the organization's magazine and electronic and print newsletters. The AHBA also provides an array of services like health insurance and small business services.

www.workingsolo.com

This is the site of Working Solo, Inc., a creator of seminars, tapes, books, and other information on working from home.

www.hoaa.com

Also known as "SOHO Central," this is the Web site of the Home Office Association of America, a nonprofit organization for home-based entrepreneurs.

www.smalloffice.com

This is the web site of *Small Business Computing & Communications* and *Home Office Computing* magazines, two of the lengthiest-published titles in the genre.

Design
Find a Space and Make It Work

Location, location, location. Even established entre-preneurs get tripped up on the best location for the home office. Think about where your office should be and how its presence there will affect—and be affected by—the dynamics of the home and work setting. Before deciding on where your office should be, review every available room in your home and make an educated, well-thought-out decision. Once in place and furnished, home offices are hard to relocate.

Avoid chaos. Where's the nerve center of your business going to be? I hope it's not where the nerve center of the household is. The best home offices operate from behind doors that close. That way, you can drown out the sounds of family, dogs, doorbells, televisions, stereos, and the assorted din of household life without miffing the family. Even if you live alone, an office set up in a spare room provides the quiet time that solo flyers come to appreciate. Closed doors also hide midweek's messy office, when the desire or rationale to clean it up just doesn't exist.

Create a transition. When you commuted, the time in the car or on the train was your transition from home to office. But the home office has no such passage to speak of. By creating a dedicated office, home-based workers are able to walk across a real threshold and create a mental and physical transition from home to place of work. They can close the door and immerse themselves in the structure and solitude of the office and become more in tune with the office mind-set.

Cop a view. The great outdoors is excellent visual and mental stimulation—certainly better than a wall. Don't tuck the office into a dark, cavernous den or the desk into a corner of the dedicated office. Take advantage of any available window, French or sliding door, or other space with a view. If office dynamics won't allow the desk to be set neatly into such a space, just make sure you've got a bit of a glimpse of something other than walls.

Stifle the ruckus. Offices with windows facing the front yard help entrepreneurs see, greet, and/or avoid potential disturbances—delivery men, family, salespeople, etc.— whose arrival could awaken children, cause dogs to bark, or otherwise cause a ruckus. If it's a parcel being delivered (and you have standing orders with the delivery company to leave a package at the doorstep), you'll know you don't have to jump when the doorbell rings. Windows also let entrepreneurs who are good citizens keep an eye on the neighborhood. Offices with windows facing back or side yards let work-at-home parents watch the children at play.

Don't get unnerved by ingress/egress. Beware setting up the home office near a door leading to the yard. The ease of exit for the solo flyer's soul needing brief escape to the yard will be offset by spoiled dogs and children who will become bothersome with their demands to go out—or come in—with great frequency.

Make a space to meet clients/customers. The first question should be, does your municipality allow clients or customers to visit the home office? If yes, then consider a home office large enough to accommodate a small meeting table. Or set up a comfortable meeting area in the home to entertain or meet with customers. Just make sure it's remote enough—or that meetings are scheduled when the kids are at school—so home life distractions don't interrupt the meeting itself.

Go executive. If your community or local zoning ordinances don't allow on-site meetings, then consider renting space from an executive suite or telework center. These emerging styles of business centers provide workspace, telephone answering and reception, copying, fax, and secretarial services to road warriors or home-based workers who otherwise would have no place to work or meet with customers. They also provide a bona fide business address for certain professionals to register their business if laws or regulations forbid using a residential address on a formal document. Executive suites typically provide small conference rooms or meeting space as part of the monthly rental fee. Or you can rent the space on an as-needed basis.

Pick out your antipandemonium point. If you can't afford a spare room but also can't stand the chaos, then perch the office in a remote corner of your abode. Corners of kitchens, living rooms and dens, or any common rooms are not bona fide offices (and often are not tax deductible as such). And they do little to curb the chaos that comes with a bustling household. So don't improvise unless space limitations demand it. By finding a remote locale for your "office," you'll have a solitary place to operate the business. And when guests or family come by—and they will—you'll be a gracious host who will let them have the run of your place without disrupting your work life.

Create portable transitions. If your office occupies the corner of a larger room, create separation—even a temporary one—by a room divider, a tapestry hung from the ceiling, or a Japanese shoji screen. This will establish both a visible barrier between you and the household during business hours and hide a messy office from a visitor's view. What's more, since "workaholism" is a real issue for the work-at-home professional (see chapter entitled "Health"), removing the office from your own view after hours might help avoid the temptation to return to the office for "just a few more minutes," which sometimes can lead to hours of after-hours work.

Tuck it away. If you're in a bind for space, wide or walk-in closets make good desk and computer hideaways. Organize closets to organize the business. If structured well, they can make for great workplace and storage space. When maximized, closets can provide ample storage space for papers, files, periodicals, hard goods, even computer hardware—and help you capitalize on peak performance. And because of their location in a home, closets are also perfect for storing sensitive goods—printer or fax paper, toner cartridges, and stationery, for example—away from the elements (heat and humidity) and the kids.

Avoid double-duty. Just like a bonafide home office, a closet that works well for office supplies shouldn't be used for stashing clothes or nonbusiness goods, too, or it can create a cluttered environment and will likely eliminate any possible tax deductibility.

Plan to grow. Buying or building furniture for the office is a tricky thing. No sooner does your furniture arrive than you think of something you forgot. Got room for your computer and printer on the desk today? What about a fax machine, scanner, or photocopier? Will your office setup accommodate those pieces of hardware? Don't say you'll never need that stuff; prices are falling so quickly that entrepreneurs who did without because they couldn't afford the hardware a few years ago are reading the ads every Saturday hoping to cop a great deal. If you're smart, you will have designed hardware acquisition into your schematic.

Kill the glare. Position the computer monitor so that glare from office lights or from the sun beaming through a window won't shine directly on it. Morning and afternoon sunlight can wreak havoc on computer work. If it's unavoidable, install shades, blinds, or draperies.

Don't skimp on your chair. Possibly the single most important piece of furniture in the office is the office chair. Never suffer the kitchen chair or a worn-out, hand-me-down office chair. Invest in a swivel chair on wheels to scoot around your office. Keep a keen eye out for ergonomics (see chapter titled "Health"). A good chair should be adjustable when you're seated, provide good support for your arms and lower back, and have at least five casters for base support. It should adjust for height, pitch, and back alignment and promote a "lazy" S-shaped curve where the upper back is curved slightly outward, the lower back curves in, and the base of the spine curves out. All this for $100 on up. Long hours spent in well-designed, comfortable chairs will avoid long hours at the chiropractor.

Don't cramp your style with a small desk. Choose a desk with plenty of countertop and drawer space. Need some privacy for your goodies or business ledger? Get a desk with at least one locking drawer. Will the desk or workstation accommodate your computer, printer, and fax machine? Will desk enclosures or closets hide expensive hardware—both from guests and unwanted voyeurs peeking in from outside?

Lightin' up. Plenty of good lighting—from lamps and windows—does wonders for the eyes and mind. Overhead lights illuminate the entire workspace, while softer task-focused lighting from a desk lamp can shine a direct light on the work at hand. Avoid heat-producing halogens, which give bright white light but can quickly warm a room. Also shy away from fluorescent lights, which can cast a yellowish glow and make everything—including your spirits—dour and melancholy. Instead, use incandescent and full-spectrum lights that glow with the spirit of natural lighting. Try beginning the day—especially one that starts before sunrise—with a soft task-focused lamp; then move to natural light from the window. Nights, which can be spent cleaning off the desk and filing paperwork, can be lit with an overhead light source, like a light kit on a ceiling fan, which will cool the office and add motion.

Kids and Family

Balance Work and Personal Life under One Roof

For work-at-home parents and spouses, it all starts at home. How successful you are at merging home and office depends on your mindset. And your success as an entrepreneur may depend on how successful you are at bringing often opposing forces of business and kids into line in both your home and your office. Similar to making the transition from traditional to home office, the interaction of home office and family takes some getting used to. But humans are the most adaptive species on the planet. Take advantage of what evolution has given you and adapt positively to your surroundings.

Think positively. Working with kids around the house can be done. Sure, kids can be rambunctious little imps prone to pull on those neat little wires beneath your desk or let forth a shrill cry when you're on the phone trying to convince some potential client that you are (or were) the right vendor for the job. But they're part and parcel of the work-at-home gig—and the work-at-home parent.

Take one more look at what you're getting into.
Make sure you've *really* thought out how—and if—kids will
fit into your work style. If you're convinced you can handle
this working-from-home-with-kids thing, then go at it with
fierce passion. This work style isn't for the faint of heart. You
will encounter jealously, resentment, awe, and, yes, understanding from those you meet each day.

Create your own model. Home officing creates a new
kind of home life for mom, dad, and junior, which requires a
new kind of modus operandi when work-at-home parents
interact with clients in the traditional office. Many see fit to
forewarn their clients and customers about what they'll be
facing. Others prefer to keep it quiet until the day the cat—
or kid—gets out of the bag (and one just might). Think
through how you're going to treat this. Maybe go through
your client list and choose those who you know will understand your work situation. Then tell them, so they don't get
shocked by a screaming kid down the road. Others may not
take the concept too well. So mum might be the best course.

Be the judge. If you're selling or conducting business
with high-octane corporate execs, a screaming kid in the
background might—or might not—be tolerated. Conduct
your business on a situation-specific basis. If the kids are
out of control one afternoon, then maybe a cold call or discussion with an unwitting client should be saved for another
time. Read the writing on each wall you encounter, and gov-
ern yourself accordingly.

Foster and demand your family's respect. Your home
office, your working there, and the hours you keep all
require respect from those around you. Just because you're

working from a home office doesn't mean you're able to hit the park, a movie, the beach, or some other diversion at two o'clock in the afternoon. If you're busy when friends and family drop by—and they will—kindly send them away. Or give them the newspaper to read, or the family phone to use—anything so they're not bothering you. Even the mate or children will hit you up for the occasional jaunt away from the office. If you can't break away, say so. And don't be bashful. This isn't some sidelight. This is a business you're running here. Be strong. They'll learn.

Use teamwork to promote success. Some work-at-homers work with their spouse, and some don't. Regardless of their direct influence, significant others and kids can have a major impact on your bottom line. How your loved ones treat and respect the home-based enterprise will reflect on the image you present to the business community outside. It even will affect your own mindset; if they respect what you do, you'll be more proud of what you do and strive to work that much harder. You'll feel you're an integral part of business and family, and will work harder to contribute to both. It can be a fulfilling cycle.

Enlist help from your mate, partner, or significant other. A mate (regardless of legal category) has a vested interest in your success. Enlist his or her understanding of, and support for, your enterprise. Does your mate have skills (bookkeeping, invoicing, filing, or recordkeeping) that can help you do what you do? If not, teach your mate to handle certain rote chores and thus shoulder some of the burdens of home office management while removing them from your schedule. And the mate might even qualify for a paycheck and some company benefits.

Make your mate your watchdog. Give your mate the authority to make you toe the line when you're not achieving self-set goals. Schedule meetings to outline your next week's or next month's goals, then require your mate to hold you to them. Spend some time alone together at year-end to peer into the next year. If your mate knows what you're expecting of yourself, he or she will be better able to help you meet those goals.

Expect change when you're expecting a baby. Are you working from home and expecting your first child? Setting up a new at-home business often works well for expectant parents—or for those with infants and toddlers—who have played "what if." Imagine how your specific job will be affected by the multiple breaks (feeding, diaper changes, recess, and activities) young children require during the day. Can you break away for the requisite 30-minute feedings of a newborn or infant?

Set your boundaries. Set relatively firm rules as to when the kids are to steer clear of the office. Establish guideposts for family-workplace interaction. Setting up expectations helps everybody understand his or her place and what's expected. The less ambiguous, the better on everyone. During morning or evening downtime, for example, children's presence might not be disturbing. During peak productivity, though, they could bring chaos and mental confusion. Base your guidelines on specific times of day and your performance and deadline needs.

Juggle. When kids share the home with a business, a flexible schedule is a more productive one. Early birds and night owls get work done with fewer interruptions—especially when kids are around. Juggle your schedule to rise before or "set" after they do. An added benefit: the phone rings less at odd hours, providing more quiet time to concentrate.

Post a No Trespassing sign. When the office is off limits, hang a Do Not Enter sign or a circle with a slash on the door. And close it. Too much for youngsters to comprehend? If they enter while you're on the phone with a client, a finger to the lips—or pointed out the door—might suffice as a command. For kids under four, the denial of entry might be too much to handle. Be prepared for them to refuse, cry, or pull a tantrum. Hurt feelings may need assuaging once the phone call is through.

Don't sweat the guilt. You're not a bad parent if you insist your children leave for a few moments during an important telephone call or when you're deep in thought on a project. They will eventually learn to respect your need for momentary, or stretches of, solitude. But until then, an occasional stern warning could be all it takes to get little ones to leave the office. Yes, that could elicit woeful cries. But once that stage of the project is completed, you'll set aside the papers or dim the computer monitor, head out to where your progeny are playing, and bond as if the warning never happened. Amazing thing about young kids: they forget such episodes rather quickly. Once they get older, they'll walk about quietly, more fully respecting the office scene. And you'll be that much prouder of them for it.

Lock 'em out. A well-sealed door with a solid core— maybe with an occasionally used lock, too—can work wonders to muffle kids' audible emissions, including their laughter and cries, or the noises from the television or stereo. It also helps contribute to office sanity.

"Dedicate" to save your sanity. Aside from being a tax deduction, a dedicated business telephone can set yet another boundary between your home and office. With no business calls coming across the family line, the confusion and embarrassment of kids answering clients' calls becomes a rarity, although sometimes your spouse or older kids can answer the business line when you're busy.

Decide who can answer the phone. If you're trying to appear professional, then train the family how to answer the business line appropriately—if at all. A spouse can sound like a receptionist or employee by answering, "ABC Product Corporation," which can help the business appear larger than it is.

Beware children answering the business line at any time! For those businesses whose customers and clients know it's run from home, a child's reply can add levity to the day and create an icebreaker for fresh conversation. Not everyone is so understanding, though, especially if the child can't carry on a conversation. Rule of thumb: If you know of at least one client who won't tolerate a child on the other end of the line, or if your children can't take a reliable, basic message, don't let your children answer the phone at all.

Hang 'em high. Watch where the phone is hung. If kids shouldn't be answering the telephone, it's important to make sure the phone is not where they can reach it. Keep the business line in the office. If the family and business share a line that rings in the kitchen, bedroom, or common areas, either turn off those phones during business hours or put them where the kids can't get to them.

Time shift. Power on and take advantage when the kids nap. Get the kids into a nap routine. Shift your work schedule to accommodate a child's wake-time habits. Work when they sleep, are at school, out with friends, or doing homework.

Give candy to a baby. Store toys in a desk drawer or desk-side box to keep kids busy. Keep especially enticing toys or snacks hidden and close at hand as emergency distractions during important phone calls. For those kids who won't take the hint or command, stash candy or a toy nearby and offer it up in exchange for their silence. At the very least, young ones will be quiet as they partake of the offering.

Let the little ones play copycat. Keep colored markers, crayons, scrap paper (a good way to recycle old faxes and letters), and the like for the kids to color on. Just make certain that their paper pile is nowhere near yours and that they don't end up writing on that report you were polishing. Maybe buy or build a little desk to keep in the office. It expands their imagination by letting them make believe they're working but also keeps them quiet when you're working and they're around.

Teach them a lesson. Aside from being a great way to raise kids, working from home provides an opportunity to teach some lessons you can't give from a downtown tower. Not only does working from home teach your children about what you do for a living, they will see the process of work. Think of it as a daily episode of "Take Our Children to Work Day."

Put 'em to work. Let them stuff envelopes, lick stamps, or put books or phone books away. As they get older, their responsibilities can grow. It eliminates the negative emotion of having to be kicked out of the office (though that is a necessary evil at times). And if you pay them, it can teach them the value of working.

Can't mute the kids or TV? Mute the phone. A telephone mute button can hide a dog's barks or a child's cries—at least briefly. With a sixth sense, you'll learn to anticipate a bark or a child's request for a snack while you're on the phone, and you'll become a quick trigger on the mute switch. You'll also be able to mute your own replies—and, yes, reprimands—when the citizenry outside the office get a little too noisy for the worker.

Schedule play dates. Team up with other at-home parents to get the children out of the home—or to have other kids over and keep your child's focus off you. What's more, by getting into a regular play routine with two other families, for example, your home office will be quiet two out of three days. This works especially well with children who attend school or preschool together. That way, you won't even have to leave the house to drive the car pool on the playmate's day to entertain.

Know when to say, "It's time." Even if child rearing were the intent of the at-home business, admit when the little ones are just too much to manage alone. Investigate an au pair, day care, preschool, a young "mother's helper" for after school or a teen for the summer or during vacation periods. The money you'll earn by being able to be more productive often can more than offset the cost of child care. Besides, when your mind is clearer because you've been able to focus on your work instead of getting frustrated with the kids, you'll appreciate each other's company that much more.

Your kids will only be young once. Part of the joy of being a work-at-home parent is having time for your children. Though the goal is to grow your business and be successful, remember to call it quits at a reasonable hour to leave time for family. You can always go back to the office later once all are asleep. And when possible, indulge. Blow out early on a lazy Friday and take the family to the park or a movie. When they're older, your children will remember both the times they were standing outside the door as you slaved away in the home office, as well as the weekday jaunts to the park. Those are fond memories that work-at-home parents can create.

Time

This Ain't Some Nine-to-Five Gig, So Set Your Work Clock

Forget the nine-to-five clock. This isn't even eight to six. In the home office, work shifts to meet schedules, deadlines, whims, and personal peak performance. The traditional five 8-hour workdays a week have become seven 24-hour workdays a week by availability. Take your biological prime time to the next level by coming to know and understand how you work—physically and metaphorically. After awhile, you'll come to know that your engine will lose steam by 9 PM, and you'll be better off hitting the sack and setting the alarm for 5 AM, or that you're a night owl who can brew some java and work 'til 3 AM. Reintroduce yourself to yourself.

Capitalize on time. Time is the only commodity you cannot buy more of. The better you capitalize on what you've got, the more productive and successful you'll be.

Set your circadian rhythm. If night owls and early birds do get work done with fewer interruptions, then fiddle with your internal clock. Some people rise before the sun and work through the day. Others wake late and work late.

Others conform to a traditional day—capitalizing on those hours when traditional workers can be reached in their offices. If you find you could use a little more quality quiet time at the home office, experiment for two weeks. First, try waking early and hitting the office before the business day starts to hum. Then, the next week, try staying in the office after the traditional workday is through, again appreciating the quiet that comes from working a flexible shift. Determine what works best for you.

Determine and capitalize on your biological prime time. When are your best times to work on the computer, make telephone calls, or be creative? Do you need to spend this Wednesday calling clients and sources around the country? Should Thursday evening be spent working on the computer with some soft music playing in the background? Some people who have limited client contact (on either a daily basis or project by project) work best with an eclectic schedule. They may, for example, work from dawn 'til noon, break for a few hours, and return later in the afternoon to work in solitude and silence as the phone ceases and the brain hums along. Office hours can be as pliable as words yet to be put to a blank page. Make of them what you need them to be. Still . . .

Establish contact time. For the sake of traditional workers and clients, create firm work hours when they can call you. Even though you are a solo flyer prone to individuality, clients may get unnerved if they never are able to get you on the phone. That doesn't mean such hours can't be set to harmonize with your own biological work routine. It's just that once you've cast the schedule, your body and brain—and your clients—will appreciate the structure.

Apply flextime. Be flexible as needs change. If one day calls for business—or some personal—errands, take the time and run about town. Then be prepared to make up for lost time in the office that night. Nine-to-five can easily be shifted to seven-to-midnight. And by working when the phones aren't ringing, you'll be that much more productive.

Synchronize your home and office rhythms. Merge your own prime time with your household's dynamics. Wake early to take advantage of the settling quiet of your home before the family rises. Once the commotion begins, take a break to shift the household into second gear. When the rush hour is over, shift yourself into third gear and hum through 'til lunchtime. Downshift for a meal, and rev back up again for the afternoon rush. When the household bustle begins anew, downshift once more to merge with the new traffic. When the day's done and the "interstate" is clear, set the business on cruise control and work on a newly cleared highway. In other words, adapt.

If appropriate, set aside time to *not* answer calls. This fosters uninterrupted time—especially when you're on a tight deadline—and allows you to complete tasks without breaking concentration. Better still, screen calls with an answering machine or caller ID if you're expecting an important call.

Be off work but not out of touch. Use voice mail to announce your schedule to the outside world. When setting aside "out-of-touch" work time, leave a message saying, "I'll be out all morning on Monday, returning this afternoon." Always let people know your schedule and that you'll be checking in or returning calls immediately on your return to the office.

Come to know your seasonal cycles. In the beginning, any client who came through the door at any time was good. First-time clients had no schedule or cycle that you could predict. They were responding to your marketing efforts, some good PR, or a referral that made the connection. But once the business cycle matures, it ebbs and flows in an almost predictable rhythm. Learn, anticipate, and respond to those cycles and you'll be able to gear up for boom times and downshift for lean periods. You'll acquire supplies, alert vendors, and put subcontractors on notice that they should be expecting the appropriate cycle.

Understand your seasonal whims and know your finances better. Are certain times of the year your boom times, while others are slow as molasses? Then set aside some extra finances in the bankbook to get you through until things pick up.

Use seasonal downtime for your vacation. Your busy season is no time for a vacation. Schedule time away during the slow months of your profession. That way, you're likely to miss less work or fewer client calls for business.

Valuate your time. Working solo is a matter of managing and maximizing your time, prioritizing your tasks, and outsourcing when workloads peak. Delegating responsibility is one of the most difficult tasks for an entrepreneur because most think they're the best at what they do. Get over it! You may be right, but does packaging goods, addressing envelopes, filling out invoices, or some other mindless chore demand perfection? Besides, what do you value or charge for an hour? Do you think having a temp or a family member handle a rote chore costs less? You betcha!

Farm out rote chores. Take five rote chores and farm them out to the spouse, the kids, a part-timer, or a home-based secretarial service. The time saved can be turned into more profitable functions.

Outsource during peak periods. Put a price on what you do, then calculate what it would cost for you to personally deliver a package to a client during a peak period, for example, as opposed to having a courier deliver it for you. Delegation of work is a learned skill that makes an effective chief executive effective. Besides, if you priced the project correctly, courier fees were already worked into the bid.

Use a computer program to track your time. Software today drives the efficient home-based business. Some programs will let you divide your time into billable and non-billable hours, which not only lets you know how much you should be charging a client for a job but also lets you better gauge your own time management.

Tools
Arm Yourself for Success

A craftsman is a worker who uses tools to ply a trade. But what's the cost of *not* having the right tools? You may be a savvy business person, but without that assistant who greased the wheels in the corporate office, you're left on your own to make the business run smoothly. It's tangible and intangible tools that make the machine work. With a computer and laser printer, you can make overhead transparencies for a speaking engagement—for far less cost and with easier alterations—than if you relied on a local copy center or service bureau to create such video aids for a hot presentation. Similarly, a good plain-paper fax machine will allow you to make single photocopies when you need to return a contract to a client but want a copy for your records. The business or marketing plans outline where you anticipate your business being tomorrow.

College Economics 101 no doubt mentioned the principle of cost-benefit analysis. Figure out what you're spending on outside service versus how much money, time, aggravation, and speed-to-market you'd gain with an investment in technology.

Don't bleed on the leading edge. If you are an early adopter, someone who needs the latest hardware and software from the "bleeding edge" of technology, it's going to cost you. The latest PC or Macintosh, the best scanner, the hottest desktop photocopier all cost *big* money. Problem is, many of the tools we already own do the job just fine, thank you. And if your high-quality printing needs are infrequent, why buy the highest-performing printer if you can just take a diskette to the local copy center and have it output for a couple of bucks?

Bundle your imaging needs. Today's multifunction machine — printer/fax/scanner/copier/fax-modem — saves money over buying its individual components. The multifunction machine comes with integrated software to provide compatibility and user friendliness—and killer image manipulation—to the show. It even saves desktop space. Just beware one downside: If any one feature goes, the whole enchilada goes in tow to the shop, which could put the company imageless during repair downtime.

Get online. Not online yet? Why not? Cost certainly isn't the issue, with modems less than $100 and Internet access less than $20 a month. The research capabilities of the Internet and the immediacy and growing use of electronic mail for business and personal applications make connecting an essential process. (See the chapter titled "Connecting.")

Become a media hound. Keep up on the local news and subscribe to those trade journals—they're tax-deductible brain food. Looking for even more good info on business? Request the Consumer Information Catalog that's always advertised on television. Write the Computer Information

Center, 7D-7, PO Box 100, Pueblo, CO 81002. It's loaded with info on free and inexpensive publications related to small business. Topics include patents and copyrights, establishing credit, small business management, and starting a business. You can view all these publications at the Consumer Information site at www.pueblo.gsa.gov. Best of all, the catalog is free.

Stock up on reference tools. Remember that *World Book Encyclopedia* you slaved over as a kid? Today it's on CD-ROM with similar products on the Web. So, too, are dictionaries, thesauri, atlases, and other reference books—all packaged into single software bundles. Build and frequent a digital and paper-bound home office reference library of books germane to your spoken tongue and your trade. Paper books are important to own for easy reference when your computer is turned off.

Rip out and stash. Build a reference library of pertinent articles from your flow of periodicals. Create a file for each subject area (or break deep subjects into small, more manageable categories), and fill them with good reference articles. Don't forget to write the date of publication on the article (time reference is important). Then write the date and article name on the cover of the folder for easy reference.

Exchange directories. Do you often need telephone numbers of companies or people in New York, or an address in L.A.? Get friends in other cities to mail you their old telephone books (in exchange for your doing the same)—especially if you use long-distance directory assistance frequently. At nearly a buck a call, the postage can be offset quickly. Need an area code for a city in another state? Call the operator (not directory assistance). It's usually a free call.

Log on to directory assistance. Trying to find out who belongs to a phone number? Searching for a phone number? Try www.555-1212.com/white_us.htm. Looking for a business listing? Log on to GTE Corporation's "SuperPages" business directory (superpages.gte.net/).

Clear your desk and travel light and in-the-know. Bulky, cumbersome, picture-filled date books consume valuable desk real estate. Go mini. A small, 3-by-6-inch date book can be stashed neatly on a corner of the desk or on the reference shelf. Or it can hit the road in a jacket pocket, satchel, or briefcase. Because they're available in daily, weekly, or monthly layouts, small date books will conform to your needs.

Need a PDA? The latest in technological tools, the Personal Digital Assistant (PDA) is a small, handheld organizer that can carry names, telephone numbers, and addresses as well as write letters and store other database information. It can hook up to a cellular telephone to send or receive faxes or e-mail, and some can link to your PC or laptop to upload or download your contact information. Electronic organizers take a "byte" out of chaos. One downside to helping both organize and make portable PDAs or contact management software in computers is that to access the data, the assistant or computer needs to be turned on. While that's not an issue for the PDA, it can become a minutes-long wait for the PC while the software boots up. Still, love 'em or hate 'em, PDAs and contact management software can store more info—and in a smaller space in the case of a PDA—than a gross of little black books and calendars could ever fathom. Just make sure the info is downloadable to your computer (and that you do it—regularly). Get used to the PDA; it's the tool of tomorrow.

Keep your numbers separate. If you write your telephone numbers in a date book, be prepared to transfer a batch of digits at year's end. Instead, buy a separate little black book. It shares all the attributes of the date book, without the burden of rewriting everything when the New Year comes.

Never scratch out old names and numbers; erase. Clients move, businesses move, people move. Ink is forever. Learn to write in pencil and keep the chicken scratch out of your address book.

Build a killer Rolodex or telephone number system. Many people deal with businesses by category and not by individual. So organize your personal telephone directory by categories, with numerous names and contacts under a given heading. Names of people or organizations might belong under two categories, making it easier to not forget where they were placed in the first place.

Keep two Rolodexes. A good Rolodex or contact management software system will grow quickly. Maybe dedicate one Rolodex or contact category subject heading for individuals or single businesses that don't belong in a broader category. A second can be used for the category or group listings. This way, as the entries grow, you minimize the time spent looking through a large system by already having divided it in two.

Make it personal. Include important personal and business information about your client in your Rolodex or your contact management software. Certainly, a secretary's name is important; it earns points with the second most important person on that entry (some might argue the secretary or assistant is *the* most important contact because he or she is the gatekeeper). But what about your contact's wife's or kids' names and birthdays, their alma maters, their favorite pastimes. Do they like a certain cigar, vacation getaway, or restaurant? Remember their special days or events and you'll endear yourself to them. Best of all, they'll think you simply cared enough to make a mental note.

Create your own small business dossier. Tools are more than tangible things. Any small business should have a dossier of files on itself, which will help guide it and its operations over the life of the business. You might think you know where you want your business to go. But if you put your thoughts in writing, you'll have a paper trail laid out for your direction and how you're going to get there. What's more, creative thinking can breed on itself. As you're putting your thoughts to paper, more will come to mind, and the documents—the business plan, mission statement, growth and marketing plans—will take on very real lives of their own.

Create a business plan. The first file for the dossier, aside from business licenses or articles of incorporation, should be the business plan. A business plan will help you chart the course of your business, your sales and marketing agendas, and your performance goals for the next one, three, and five years. It can be a blueprint for your success and a road map to follow or to chart your missteps. And if you seek funding, it's a document most lenders would like to see.

Create a mission statement. Right beside your business plan should be your mission statement. This details in a sentence or two what your company's goal(s) is (are). Make it pithy and poignant, then print and post it in the office. Don't have a wall to post it on? Go into your computer's program manager and turn it into the text for your screen saver. Print it small and tape it below the screen of your computer monitor or laminate it and place it on your desk. Read it regularly like a mantra.

Plan your growth with a growth plan. Where do you want to be tomorrow or next year, and how are you going to get there? You'll never know unless you put it in writing and get it posted. What do you want your sales volume to be? What do you want to be charging for your work? How many employees do you want to have? Short-term and long-term goals should be clearly defined. Remember: Each milestone is different for each company, each entrepreneur, and each industry. Toe your own line.

Sell yourself with a marketing plan. A marketing plan is an outline of how you intend to pitch and sell your product or service. It's essential to successful marketing efforts. How are you going to sell your product or service? Are you going to dabble in public relations, maybe place a print ad or two, speak at some local events or organizations? All are good ideas. But if you don't put them to paper as a cogent and understandable marketing formula, your effort will come out more like a shotgun blast than a finely sighted sniper's shot to your target audience. Whether it's a start-up or a business long past its honeymoon, a marketing plan will help define the media you've chosen to get your word out, the timetable by which you intend to implement all this, and what you've budgeted for each facet of the marketing campaign. (It *will be* an orchestrated, ongoing effort—a campaign as outlined in the "Marketing" chapter—won't it? Anything less could be a futile waste of time, effort, and resources.) Be detailed and thorough—and nimble enough to change as new opportunities arise.

Resolve to make promises. Some people aren't big on New Year's resolutions. But for the solo flyer, the end of the year—or any moment the spirit moves you for that matter— is a great time to make a few business promises. What products do you want to introduce and when? If you are a service provider, what clients would you like to woo and win? Clearly outline a half-dozen reasonable goals in the order of their importance to you or the future of the business. Then, like the mission statement, post them in your office where you can see them regularly (the wall or desktop might get crowded, but it's a "good crowded"). Realize that all your promises may not come to fruition, but strive to achieve as many as possible. Then, keep a fat red Sharpie pen in the pencil drawer or cup and cross them out when they've been conquered.

Contact your local Small Business Development Center. This federal agency was created to offer free advice and assistance in running a business. Learn how to launch, sustain, or expand your business. The Small Business Administration's SBA Online (www.sbaonline.sba.gov) provides scads of useful information, including an outline for a business plan. With more than 1,000 offices nationwide, these centers are reflections of the local communities in which they're based, providing workshops, seminars, and classes on topics pertinent to a given locale. These centers are a valuable resource—one that you've already paid for with your (quarterly estimated) tax dollars. So put them to good use.

Extend your resources at your state university or county extension service. These facilities, which are associated with state-run universities, have micro business departments that provide classes, networking groups, literature, and various insights into working alone or launching a business. Many also have access to business school instructors who help guide fledgling entrepreneurs through that maze of business start-up and maintenance.

Find an experienced mentor in the community. Many retired, active, or older executives, college business professors, or volunteer counselors are willing to provide their insights to help budding businesses. All a professor might ask for in return is that you serve as an example for his or her class. SCORE, the Service Corps of Retired Executives (www.score.org/), is brimming with one-time execs who have volunteered to become business coaches with aspiring entrepreneurs in their local community. They're also called counselors to America's small businesses, and their Web site offers tips, case studies, success stories, e-mail counseling, and online workshops.

MORE TOOLS FOR YOUR DOSSIER

The Internet and World Wide Web nicely round out any small business dossier. Between online resource tools and search engines, which ferret out Web sites pertaining to specific topics on the Internet, you'll have plenty of research material for your next project or proposal.

www.m-w.com
Merriam Webster's online "The Language Center" even provides synonyms.

www.thesaurus.com
Roget's Thesarus: search electronically if you're looking for that one special alternative word.

www.refdesk.com

"My Virtual Reference Desk" offers scads of information on scores of topics. *Very deep* and a quality addition to any cyber reference library.

www.columbia.edu/acis/bartleby/bartlett

Bartlett's Familiar Quotations: from Newton to Shakespeare to modern orators and thinkers, search by topic or word for a quote for every occasion.

www.fedstats.gov

Find a plethora of federal statistics and demographics here that are perfect for small business research.

www.census.gov

Census Bureau home page: find information about the population, people, and demographics of the United States.

www.hotbot.com

The HotBot search engine from Wired Digital searches for URLs, e-mail addresses, news sites, usenet groups, and media, culture, and entertainment sites.

www.profusion.ittc.ukans.edu

Profusion simultaneously searches nine popular Web search engines, including Alta Vista, Excite, HotBot, InfoSeek, Lycos, Magellan, OpenText, WebCrawler, and Yahoo.

www.metacrawler.com

A multiengine service, Metacrawler will search multiple search engines to locate topical info for the user.

www.dogpile.com

Like Metacrawler, this quizzically named engine will search multiple engines like Yahoo or Lycos and return a more comprehensive listing of info. Remember to mark "usenet" in your query, and both Meta and Dogpile will search those groups for info as well.

www.internets.com

This site reports results of searches of hundreds of major databases for valuable information on an eclectic array of topics. It also provides one of the Web's largest collections of direct links to online databases.

www.internet.org

This site lets you search to see if a specific Web site is registered to another user (even if it doesn't come up as part of an Internet site search).

www.four11.com

This Yahoo-owned site is ideal for finding people and provides an effective search of Internet e-mail addresses.

www.worldpages.com

Worldpages will search for people's telephone numbers in other countries.

Marketing

Sell Yourself and Your Business Effectively

Marketing is getting remembered. Whether it's through a direct mail campaign, cold calls, a Web site, fancy stationery, or speaking at events, the *only* point of successful marketing is getting remembered so people will want your product or service. It easily is the most important part of any business: Don't sell today, don't get paid tomorrow.

That said, we'll delve a little more deeply here to learn how to plan your business life—and personal life, for that matter—to maximize selling your product and yourself. Being a salesman of the business, your success depends on you. Carry business cards, product samples, and a healthy dose of buoyant optimism everywhere you go. Take it to the next level. Never let a good marketing opportunity pass you by.

Market or die. Home-based businesses operating on paper-thin margins have little room for error. If you don't sell something today, tomorrow you'll go without. So sell! Market yourself to everyone around you—existing clients, potential clients, friends of existing or potential clients. Everyone is a potential prospect. Break out your pan and start prospecting.

Keep it clear. Using your marketing plan, create a clear image and message. Part of any marketing presentation should be a clear branding or positioning statement about your product or service. That way, when you begin to create that hot new brochure, Web site, business card, stationery, or advertisement, each complements the other and promotes a common theme. It's very easy to present a convoluted and disjointed marketing position. Stay focused—in theme, color, graphical treatment, and even typeface or wording style.

Create more than a one-shot pony. A marketing "campaign" is called a campaign for a reason. From printed ads to press releases or e-mail contact, repetition gets remembered. And the point of marketing is not just to get an article written today. It's to become a reporter's resource or a potential client's vendor tomorrow.

Recognize the disciplines' differences. Advertising, public relations, sales, and promotion are vastly different types of marketing. Advertising typically is spending money or otherwise getting space in a medium like a newspaper or newsletter, or on a radio or television station. Public relations is convincing an editor or writer from one of those media to do a story on you. Sales is what it says: selling your product or service. Promotion is getting out there and selling yourself by giving away brochures or business cards at networking activities, for example. Use each—together—effectively to create a marketing campaign that turns heads and sells you and your product or service.

Become a cunning advertiser. Many traditional corporations have deep-pocket advertising budgets. Home offices, on the other hand, need to look for ways to aggressively advertise without breaking the bank. Be sly. Find newsletters, community newspapers, or trade publications that might sympathize with your size and cut you a discount for your printed ad.

Work for ads. Some publications will run your advertisement in exchange for your writing an article on your area of expertise. Not only will this get you a free or reduced price on your ad, you'll get the additional exposure of the article (which many public relations executives say provides better bang for the marketing dollar than a paid ad because of its perceived objectivity).

Barter. Barter to boost your budget. In advertising lingo, bartering is trading ad space for the product or service of the advertiser. This works for print, newsletters, online — essentially anywhere where ad space can be purchased. Not only does bartering give the advertiser low cash exposure, because it's a product or service, the advertiser is losing the cost basis of the bartered product.

Buy remnant ads. Think display or print advertising has to be expensive? Consider creating a small ad and dropping it and a small check (say, $20) in the mail to one of your industry journals or small community newspaper. Include a letter saying how you're a start-up or SOHO business (relatively speaking, if you're past the honeymoon) and don't have a lot of money to spend. If the publications have any remnant or leftover ad space, you'd appreciate their running your ad. The potential for positive results may surprise you.

Share ad costs with complementary businesses. If you align with four other complementary businesses, you can pool your resources and each underwrite the cost of one ad. For example, a photographer, a desktop publisher, a writer, and a marketer can each put in one-fourth the cost of an ad (as well as their respective skills in creating the ad, which will save them more money in production fees) in a publication that serves each equally well. Sharing also works with brochures and other collateral material.

Go direct. Direct mail is an ideal way to hit your audience directly—with little wasted spillover into unwanted markets. Ask for the prospect's business several times in the letter and be explicit. Want a better response? Include a call to action ("Want more information? Reply today") with a SASE—a self-addressed stamped envelope with a real stamp.

Go postal. Traditional direct mail, with preprinted envelopes, letters, and first class postage, can get costly. Instead, go low-cost with a postcard. With images printed right where recipients can read them without opening an envelope, they can be more effective than letters in some cases. Inexpensive to print—especially with today's personal laser printers—a postcard campaign can be conceived, designed, printed, and executed in an afternoon. No folding, stuffing, or sealing. A mail merge function will even print your prospect's address right in place. And the results can be tracked quickly. The postal service treats postcards like regular first-class mail in handling speed at one-third the cost of a regular No. 10 envelope. Just size it right: minimum 3½ inches by 5 inches; maximum 4¼ inches by 6 inches. Even a standard 4×6-inch index card can be mailed at the postcard rate.

Get on the Web. "But everyone's there," you might claim in disdain. A Web presence is not an ad campaign. It is part of an effective sales and marketing program that puts your product or service in front of a waiting audience immediately. You can post images of your work, references from satisfied clients, white papers on your take on your industry, even statistics about your niche. Your site can become more than a marketing medium; it can make you a permanent and vibrant resource to your existing and potential customers as well as the media, all of whom might access your site, learn something new, and cite you and/or your company. Now *that's* effective marketing.

Banner banter. If your company has a Web site, re-member to exchange banners or hot-link buttons on each others' sites. This is an exceptional way to garner eyeballs from complementary sites. An easy way is to conduct a Web search to learn who's out there, and then e-mail the propri-etor about an exchange. Or you can contact a banner exchange company, like linkexchange.com, smartclicks. com, or Ad-Xchange (www.ad-x.com), which lets the user target geographically by zip code.

Get remembered with a novel notion. Buy or barter for advertising specialties. Ad specialties are the pens, calen-dars, paperweights, coffee mugs, mouse pads, and other goods that you always receive during the holidays and at trade shows. Just make yours useful and memorable. If you're a writer, send a pen or a feather quill and base with your name. If you run an outdoor tour operation, send a desk-mounted compass with your name, phone and fax number, and e-mail address or Web site.

Become PR savvy. Public relations and word-of-mouth endorsements are more valuable than paid advertising, and knowledgeable and well-spoken futurists are always in demand for a good quote in the media. So create happy cus-tomers who are willing to tell others (remind them to if you have to), and then get talking about yourself!

Spin the Rolodex or access Act! Once you're solo, call every person you know and let the world know! Dig deep and distant too. Don't be shy about calling on long-lost friends, family, or contacts when you promote yourself. Tell recent and long-past coworkers and former corporate clients that you're on your own and offering up your services.

Tell the 'hood. Tell your neighbors that you work from home. They'll feel the neighborhood is safer during the day, and you might get new business leads. Stay versed in the politics of work-at-home in your community. Be a conduit for change in the work-at-home arena.

Ferret out the local angle. Every national or international story has a local angle. Make it your business to find out how the local angle involves you, and pitch yourself as a source and resource to the local—and national—media. Some of the best public relations people are those who talk a lot and have good stories to tell. And whose story is better than yours? One day your business will grow significantly enough to hire a PR firm or bring someone in-house to handle media relations. Today, doing it yourself—assuming you do it right—can lead to solid returns for less money.

Be the expert. Find a niche—or a few depending on the market—in your general area and "specialize" in it. People are not what their business card says they are. They are the skill sets they offer their clients. That said, you are an expert in your field. Yell it from the mountaintop to let those around you know.

Become a resource. PR and broadcast faxing lead to one important goal: becoming a resource people can call on for information or input on a topic you're learned in. If the local media are always looking to put a local spin on the news, offer to write articles on business topics for the local papers. Do the same for your industry trade journals or other publications.

Develop media smarts. When an event happens (e.g., you come up with a new product or study, or something happens in the news that you could lend some insight on), get the media machine rolling.

Locate the media. It's one thing to write a press release. It's another to get it to the right reporters, writers, or editors. *Bacon's Directories* (800-753-6675), *Working Press of the Nation,* (800-521-8110), and *Editor & Publisher Yearbook* (212-675-4380) each provide listings of editorial staff at U.S. media outlets—both print and broadcast. These plus other resource guides are probably available at the main branch of your public library.

Build a media contact list. Hit the local library's reference desk. Ask for directories of media outlets, reporters, and editors. Spend an afternoon flipping through them and create a database of appropriate contacts for your market. Spend another afternoon in the main library's periodical section looking at all its magazines, again writing down pertinent information from appropriate publications, including editors' names, addresses, phone and fax numbers, and e-mail addresses.

Browse and learn. Local reporters and editors like local stories. Read all of your local and regional periodicals so you know who the beat writers are and generally what the "tone" of the publication is. You want to write your release to fit the style of the particular publication.

Learn to write. The better you can write a simple press release and a mail, fax, or e-mail message, the more adept and comfortable you'll be at sending out such correspondence. Become accustomed to sending news to the media at least once a month. Include such information as how current news or your product or service affects the publication's readers. Tell editors and reporters what makes you an expert resource on your field of work and why the media should call on you—now and in the future. Be sure to include a few direct quotes so if an editor wants to use your information, it won't necessarily require a telephone call to get you to say something that can be quoted directly.

Give 'em the pix. A story that includes an attractive product shot or staged picture is more likely to get published than a story without one. The image could even be a chart or bulleted information relevant to your article or story (charts, graphs, and bulleted points can be faxed whereas pictures can't). Be prepared to e-mail or FedEx pictures to editors or reporters if they ask. In fact, don't make them ask. Offer first.

Don't be a pest. Journalists dislike (at the least) two things: calls on deadline from pesky PR people and pesky PR people who have no idea what the publication is all about. First question to ask when calling a reporter or editor: "Are you on deadline?" If the answer is yes, offer to call back. If the answer is no, be prepared to pitch your idea, specifically noting how your story will serve the publication's readers.

Bark up the right tree. Know the go-to guy. Before pitching your spiel, give a brief one-paragraph synopsis, and then ask if the reporter or editor on the other end of the line is the right person to be talking to about that topic. If the per-

son says no, ask who is. While on that call, verify the fax and
e-mail address, and inquire by which means he or she would
prefer to receive press releases. Some people are quite pro-
tective of their e-mail addresses, so don't use them without
asking.

Be in pictures. Local business television producers are
always looking for someone to have on the show. Don't ever
underestimate the value of your product or your message.
Even if the show is on public access television on the local
cable network, get on there. Your initial experiences will
break down any stage fright you might have. With each sub-
sequent appearance, you'll grow more confident. And with
each visit, you'll reinforce your message with the audience.

Generate additional publicity. Write and fax news releases to area business and community publications—and
potential clients (you might want to ask first if they mind
receiving such information). Repetition enhances readers'
memories.

Speak up. Contact business professors at area colleges
and universities and offer to lecture on business topics
related to your area(s) of expertise (never limit your subject
area). Then volunteer to speak to area civic and community
groups. After all, who are experts? Those with a business
card and newsletter proclaiming themselves to be one.

Become a broadcast faxer. Take that simple, one-page
newsletter and fax it to your current and prospective clients
and local newspapers. Include news about your industry or
area of expertise and special notes that might be important
to them.

Get electronically spry. Spend an hour or two entering all your contact names and fax numbers into the fax software's phone book "groups." That way, when you have a press release to send out, you can schedule a time (like during dinner, when you're away from the computer and the dialing won't interfere with any of your applications) and hit "send." Come back, check the send log to ensure all were sent OK and spend the next day following up with telephone calls to the recipients.

Be a broadcast e-mailer. Enter e-mail addresses by group (as with fax numbers in the phone book group section of your fax software) and disseminate. Just don't spam (or send e-mail advertisements or announcements with reckless abandon). Always ask recipients if they mind receiving such information, and then give them the opportunity to subscribe or unsubscribe easily.

Create a fax or electronic campaign. Write a series of press releases on your topic, and send them out over a few weeks or months. Remember to follow up each transmission with a phone call to ensure receipt and ask if the recipient has any questions about it. Be sure to personalize the letters—make a friend of the recipient.

Create an informative subject line. The "subject" line on electronic mail helps readers quickly sort important and superfluous e-mail. Make sure yours is on the must-read list. Instead of "Ways to Market Better," write "Hot Marketing Tips." Once readers are hooked, provide them with solid information in an easy-to-read tone, keeping the text to no more than a few paragraphs packed with tips and laden with bullets and white space that is easy on the eye and promotes quick, effective reading. Always end any correspondence with a "call to action" like "Call or reply via e-mail to ABC Home-Office Co. to learn more about how you can prosper with this unique opportunity" or "For a complete text of the preceding information, simply reply via e-mail."

Write and edit well. Don't let any spelling or grammatical errors slip through. And always make sure your name, address, and phone and fax number are included.

Put ink to paper. Electronic mail is fast, efficient, and cost effective. A fax is tangible. But a letter in the mail is tangible and memorable. It helps create an endearing connection between writer and recipient. Strive to write a few letters a week.

Send season greeting cards to clients, vendors, and new business prospects. And not just *any* season greeting cards. Stage a fun shot and have a professional photographer or even your significant other hit the shutter. Characters get remembered. Just don't run them through the postage meter. Buy memorable stamps.

Jot thank-you letters or notes. An e-mail or telephone call is nice. But they're fleeting and forgotten quickly. A note, especially one written on your attractive thank-you stationery, gets remembered.

Become a crack cold caller. Want to send shudders down a first-time marketer's spine? Mention that cold calling is the road to enhanced business opportunities. To many, the hardest thing to do in sales is to cold call. Get over it. There are only two ways to make a business grow: charge more for your existing customers (and hope they never leave you) or bring in new customers. Assuming it's a combination of the two, bringing in new customers is essential to expanding the enterprise. So considering you're going to have to make those cold calls anyway, get good at it. Practice with friends or family. Tape-record your pitch (but don't read from a script—it sounds hokey and will get picked out in a heartbeat). You'll eventually enjoy the challenge and thirst for the rewards when a prospect says yes.

Sell yourself. In a small business, no matter the product, people are buying the salesperson as much as the product. Market yourself positively and incessantly without hesitation, embarrassment, or guilt.

Carry samples. Got a few of your products or brochures in your briefcase, your trunk, your purse? If not, why not? Isn't the point to sell your wares—whenever and wherever you can? Get hawkin'! Be prepared to pitch your product, show it off, and make a sale anytime, anywhere.

Get funky. Spend time creating memorable business stationery. It'll be your look of success. A distinctive color will also help collaterals and leave-behinds stand out from the pile and it will become your calling color. Remember: Include all your contact info, including the company URL (Web site address) and e-mail address.

Deal the cards. Your business card (or your Rolodex card) is you on a two-by-three-inch scrap of paper. Make it attractive and memorable, and give them out with reckless abandon! After all, they do grow on trees, you know.

Be creative. Use the back of the card for pertinent personal info, for a product description, a picture, ordering information, a sales pitch. Or simply print "Notes" at the top and encourage recipients to use your card as a way to take notes—about you or something else important.

Plaster your name and info on everything that leaves the office. Every invoice, press release, brochure, or other correspondence that leaves the office *must* have all of your contact data on it. Your name, address, phone and fax number, and electronic mail address or Web site also should be on every leave-behind you create, including stationery, brochures, samples, even your voice mail message.

Network. Your home office can be a cocoon. Aggressive networking takes you beyond the confines of the SOHO and expands your area of influence. Meet more people, spread around the business cards, leave behind samples of your work. Join networking groups, civic organizations, chambers of commerce, business bureaus, city boards—anything to get your name and face into the community.

Attend trade fairs and business expos. Scan the Sunday or Monday business sections in the local newspapers or call the local Better Business Bureau to learn when business expos will be held in your area. Small business events often lure sole proprietors who are trying to expand their area of influence. Browse the aisles, pick up some new information, make a contact, attend some of the conferences or lectures. Hey, you might even learn something.

Ally and conquer. Expand your networking circles to form alliances with a supporting cast of characters so everyone can prosper. If you're a writer but can't draw, find an artist who can't write. If you're a photographer, ally yourself with a local dressmaker or baker, and together you can create packages for weddings and other special events. Together you can network, pitch new business, capitalize on each other's skill sets and become more things to more people.

Network with the well known, powerful, and knowledgeable. Find people knowledgeable and skilled in your area of expertise and establish a friendly working relationship with them. Apprentice with them to expand your circle of acquaintances, business contacts, or just the skill sets in your area. That way, you'll be able to capitalize on their information and enlarge your enterprise—and your horizons.

Volunteer. Being a good neighbor and corporate citizen shows you care. It also gets you out in the community and among potential clients. Just another form of networking.

Join, join, join. Becoming active in local groups gets you into circles of potential clients. Join local charity and civic boards of directors. Your codirectors often can steer business your way. Join civic associations to meet more people. Join local chambers of commerce to network and win new business. Join trade groups to learn ideas and make contacts and stay sociable.

Offer finder's fees. If friends or network compatriots steer new clients your way, reward them with a finder's fee. Either dole out a flat fee or a percentage (on a sliding scale depending on the value of the new client's business), or at least reward their effort with a gift. Consider between 5 percent and 10 percent of the first individual or year's contract plus a gift basket or other tangible thank you. It's tax deductible and memorable.

Money
Learn to Micromanage Your Cash

Income is king—and that includes what doesn't get spent. Not unlike being the owner of a large corporation, being the proprietor of a home-based business means surviving on the timely payments of your clients or customers. Being home based is the time to ditch all those wasteful, bad office habits. How you manage your financial resources between the arrival of checks can mean the difference between living comfortably and stretching money to meet month's end.

Get what you're worth. The easiest way to boost income is to raise your fee. Quite often, home-based proprietors undervalue their services because they believe clients will scoff at paying high fees to a home-based business. "How can I charge them *that* much? I work from home," the rationale goes. The real question should be: What's the quality of my work? Certainly, an office-based company charges accordingly to meet overhead. But that doesn't mean qualified executives with a strong market reputation and solid credentials—and who happen to work from home—should

52

undervalue their services because they're home based. Conduct a simple market survey. Speak with friendly competitors, with clients who know the market, with members of local, regional, or national trade associations; or read the trade journals to learn what your industry gets for your kinds of services. Charge what you believe you're worth (or what the market will bear)—sometimes more, never less.

Increasing income by cutting costs. Boosting sales is the goal of every business. But essentially the same can be achieved by reducing expenses. Cut your monthly expenses by $100 and that's the same as selling another $100 consulting session, press release, or product. Places to cut: telephone charges, unused magazine subscriptions, and even household costs that deplete the bottom line of an unincorporated business or generally sap your paycheck.

Get a raise. Hit the new guys first. New clients should bear the brunt of any scheduled fee increase, meaning if a client is accustomed to paying $100 for your product or service, and you know the market will bear $150, the existing client might scoff. New clients won't know the difference (assuming you put it in your original bid). Then, alert existing clients at your next meeting or in a telephone call that you'll be raising your rates.

Call on their dime. When calling vendors, clients, or other companies, find out if they have a toll-free number. Don't feel guilty. Just remember they created that line to facilitate sales and service for their inbound calling traffic. And it can save you ten cents a minute or more on each call.

Pitch the plastic. Many are the tales of shoestring operations that were launched with the aid of maxed-out credit
cards, eventually paying off the debt and developing the business into a colossal organization. Don't bet on it. There's a lot
of faith that solo flyers must harness to expand their companies. But high-interest credit card debt dogs the program and
weighs it down. If you must buy new equipment or make big-
ticket purchases, shop for lucrative financing terms; you'll
likely save more paying "no interest until December 1999"
than buying something now and financing it on the credit
card.

Go Bic. Now that you're paying for all your supplies,
buy in bulk from mass retailers or discount and mail order
distributors. Add your name to mail order lists so you'll know
about their sales. Hold off on purchases until sales come up.
Buy cheap. Hey, it's your money. Keep it that way.

Save yourself the trip. Delivery of catalog purchases
from major office supply retailers often is free if the purchase
is above $50 or so. Save your purchases—and time and
money, for that matter—and do your buying all at once.
Leave instructions to drop packages at your door if you don't
answer.

Post it. Don't like to drive to shop? Mail order and shop-
ping online are the time-saving waves of the future. Prices are
cheap, and service is handled from your own telephone. If
you can get around the touchy-feely-before-you-buy need,
then mail order could be the answer.

Suffer the storage, not shortages. By buying supplies in bulk, you'll save money and make fewer runs to the office supply store. And with fewer trips to the store, there will be fewer receipts to file. The only hitch: finding a place to store boxes of goods. Make sure you have an efficient and effective storage system, one that allows you to know immediately how stocks of supplies are running and where everything is.

Watch those supplies. Buying in bulk doesn't mean overstocking. Create a checklist of supplies and where they're stored. When supplies run low, buy more. But often an oversight may lead to overpurchasing, which leads to wasted money and ill-used storage space.

Recycle. Recycling isn't a cliché or something for the other guy. It's an environmentally friendly move that can save real money and make you a good corporate and community citizen. Do you use note pads for taking telephone notes, memos, or messages? Cut up those letters into reusable scratch pads. Flip over used sheets of fax or printer paper and turn them into fresh sheets of note paper. Snatch paper clips binding correspondence that comes in the mail and put them in your dispenser. When mail packaging or padded envelopes come in relatively unblemished—or at least marred in a place your mailing label or postage can cover— use them for your next outgoing parcel.

Box those files. Need storage containers for old files? Call a local printing company and get some of the boxes that their paper stock comes in. They're hearty containers with lids—and they're just the right size for storing your business-size papers or files. Or hit the local grocer for his old banana boxes. Sturdy and with firm lids, they're ideal, stackable storage units.

Use used furnishings. Speaking of recycling . . . used furniture can be a choice find indeed. Visit a local used furniture dealer, furniture rental outfit, or even a thrift shop to inquire about used desks and filing cabinets. Banks as well as insurance and other large companies will often ditch furnishings for cents on the dollar, returning outstanding quality goods (not that ready-to-assemble stuff) as they upgrade their hard goods. Just read the classifieds to learn when to be where with your checkbook in hand. Or hit the thrift store early on a Saturday to beat the masses. It may take a few visits, but the savings could well be worth it.

Trade. In-kind is cool. Advertising bartering is trading ad space for a product or service. In other areas, it's trading product for product or service for service or some mixture of the two. This is an ideal way to get the products you need without laying out cash or taking on credit debt. You need printing, and your printer needs legal services or counseling. You can even move outside the business realm. Your kid's dance class needs a brochure? Trade your services for tuition. Remember, though, dare to declare. Uncle Sam or the state revenue officer might want his share.

Take their money any way it comes. Merchant card accounts or other credit card transactions open up vast new sales avenues. Potential customers who might be slow to write a check, address and stamp an envelope, and send funds via the postal service often are more than willing to use a credit card over the telephone. But beware when lining up a merchant account: banks are cool to home-based businesses, and provider fees can be staggering if not shopped and monitored. Consider ECHO (the Electronic Clearing House at 800-233-0406), a friendly lot that typically charges less than traditional providers for Mastercard or Visa phone orders.

Make them apply for credit. Credit applications can save potential payment and collection hassles. By making new clients fill out standard applications, including client and credit references, and sign personal guarantees for debt incurred through the course of business, clients will be more likely to meet their payment obligations. If they don't pony up, you've got ample information and ammunition to use in pursuit of their debt. Still, judge each client and situation individually. You can pass on the paperwork for people you know—they're not likely to stiff you. Tell anyone else who balks at filling out your form that it's standard operating procedure for your company. If anyone hesitates further, that's bad faith and not worth the potential hassle. It makes good business sense.

"Put out a contract" on your client. Many home-based entrepreneurs scoff at contracts; too formal, they lament, or it's bad faith with the client. Forget both notions. Contracts provide a sound basis on which to do work. They outline both parties' responsibilities and expectations, and protect each in case the other has second thoughts about work or payment down the road. Further, certain aspects of a contract can be included that further solidify the arrangement, like dates of delivery, terms (especially if the job includes various stages over time), and remedies in case of default by either side. Be equitable in the contract. A purely one-sided contract . . . now that represents bad faith.

Get some up front. Home-based still means overhead. Before starting any project, request an up-front payment of between 15 percent and 25 percent on the signing of a contract. It shows good faith on your client's part and will help cover some expenses required to start a job. Once you've delivered a draft of the project, get another installment (maybe bringing the total paid up to two-thirds of the contract price). When the client is happy with the completed project, get the remainder. Remember: Financial terms must be written into your contract so there are no surprises or denials.

Offer terms. Clients like discounts, and you like getting paid and having receivables cleared off the balance sheet. Offer your clients "two-net-ten," or a 2 percent discount on balances paid within ten days. Sometimes the expediency is worth the discount (to both parties). If you're having problems collecting from someone who didn't have such an offer to begin with, offer that 2 percent discount if the balance is paid immediately.

Be a gentle "noodge." Using a tickler reminder file or simply your accounting software, schedule one hour each week to call invoiced clients to remind them payment is coming due. Start the conversation out by asking how the project is meeting their expectations or needs and if there's anything else you can do regarding the recently delivered project or new assignments coming. Then move to the reminder phase.

Call out the dogs. Be aggressive about collections. Just because you're a home-based worker doesn't mean clients can make late payments or be slow to pony up. You've sent invoices and reminders, offered terms to speed payment.

Now, don't be afraid to threaten and exercise collections procedures—though always strive to know each payer's given situation. We've all had slow months; be understanding when others face the same dilemma. Those who want to pay are embarrassed when they don't have the money to.

Know a good attorney? Even though a debtor often will pay attorney fees in collection actions, such actions can get expensive. In your networking, strive to meet an attorney specializing in small business collections. Offer to barter services for those times you need a hound to retrieve delinquent funds.

See 'em in court. You've been nice. You've tried to be understanding. But no matter what you do, the check still doesn't come. So what do you do after 90 days have passed, the client has stopped taking your calls, and still no "dinero"? Take the client to small-claims court. This avenue was almost created with the SOHO practitioner in mind. With action eligible for debts in the low thousands (depending upon the state), you don't even need a lawyer to sue. Drop $20 or so in filing fees, the debtor will be served, an appointment made, and you and your evidence will have your day in court.

Bounce back. If a client's check bounces, assess the client for the charge you'll get hit with by your bank. It could be $30 or more. If the client doesn't pay, see the preceding entry.

Beware the low bid. Keen on saving money when outsourcing? Don't always go with a low bidder—and don't bid low just to get a job. Make sure that you view the bidding process from both sides of the negotiating table. When you're the vendor, make sure that your bid includes all of your costs plus your fee and a cushion for incidentals. When you're the client, be cautious about low bids that fall too far outside the range of the other bids. Less expensive sometimes can yield lower quality—and rest assured that many potential clients have been bitten and are wary.

Become tax savvy. From your home office itself to everything you use in the daily course of affairs, learn how to use the tax code to your advantage. Stay sharp on current tax law. Don't rely solely on your accountant or other tax professional for advice. Read the tax code, formulate some ideas of what you'd like to achieve, and be an informed and knowledgeable tax citizen.

Hire a SOHO-savvy tax pro. An accountant or tax attorney skilled in, and knowledgeable of, tax code requirements affecting small businesses and home offices can be a real asset. Just make sure the accountant's philosophy about tax law mirrors your own. If you're conservative in finances, an accountant who recommends a liberal approach to tax matters will make you ill at ease. Similarly, if you're aggressive with your deductions and claims, a conservative adviser might leave you thinking you got less than you deserved.

Deduct your home office. Deducting from your annual tax return the cost of operating your home office can save paying hundreds of dollars in taxes. Deductible expenses may include monthly utilities, maintenance, and upkeep. They're bills you're going to pay anyway. Might as well get some money back. Remember: To be deductible, a home office must be "regular and exclusive," meaning you use it regularly and it doesn't double as a den or kids' playroom, for example, after hours. Always consult a tax professional about home office deductibility and tax strategy.

Don't deduct your home office. The savings gained by deducting the square footage could diminish the cost basis of your home when you sell it, meaning you'll be liable for any capital gains. And it's been said the home office deduction is a surefire "red flag" to the IRS for an audit. Regardless, consult your tax adviser.

Make sure your use jibes. Does the use stated on city occupational permits match what you've stated on your tax return? Officials often seek "concurrency in use" declarations (in other words, don't deny on an occupational license that you'll be working from home and then deduct the office on your tax return). If ignored, these issues won't go away. They may just come back to haunt you.

Get a receipt: Part I. Request, get, and keep all business-related receipts. From tolls of 25¢ to a $500 sofa for the dedicated home office, receipts are the only argument for deductibility if you're questioned by the IRS. So if you think that scrap receipt from the toll plaza isn't worth saving, just imagine a hundred of them at the end of the year—and the tax savings lost!

Get a receipt: Part II. If you live by the mantra "my canceled check is my receipt," what if your bank doesn't return your checks each month? Are you going to remember to deduct the cost of that tax-deductible product you bought?

Faithfully keep a mileage log. Mileage adds up quickly, so be good about keeping a log. Can't find a log small enough to keep on your dashboard or in the glove compartment? Buy a spiral-bound index-card book and create your own log, including date, place or person visited, purpose, beginning mileage, end mileage, and trip total. Then, when sitting in traffic, pass the time by tallying up each page's entries; this will make the year-end process easier. Also, the log, along with a date book and toll receipts, provide ample evidence of the business usage of your automobile. And don't forget: If a client reimburses you for less than the amount the IRS allows for each mile, tabulate and deduct the difference.

Make April easy. Tally expenses quarterly (preferably at the end of March, June, September, and December), and run a final total before the next quarter's first receipt is thrown into the file. That way, as you and your adviser do a midyear and year-end review and analysis, you'll know exactly where you stand—in collections and expenses.

Stash cash for the tax man. Saving for estimated quarterly tax payments is among the hardest tasks for a solo flyer. Each time a check comes in, a portion really belongs to Uncle Sam. When the checking account has a little extra in it, debit an amount you can handle without too much difficulty, and write "Blind Holdings" in the ledger entry. Use a red pen or highlighter to help remind you that it's there. Do this a few times during the quarter. Then when it's time to make your quarterly estimated payment, tally up your blind holdings, add them back to the ledger, and write out the check. It's akin to setting your clocks or watch sahead ten minutes so you're not late to meetings. You'll come to respect the running balance in your checkbook—all the while realizing the money is there when it's time to pay Uncle Sam. What's more, it provides a little cushion against overdrafts.

Dedicate and deduct. Without a dedicated business line, only long-distance calls related to business can be deducted. With a dedicated line, all bona fide business calls and the line itself can be deducted. Besides, busy home offices need a business line. Getting scads of faxes and spending time online? A dedicated fax/data line may also be deductible as long as the family isn't logging on for personal use after hours.

Don't absorb telephone taxes. If you can bill clients for long-distance telephone charges, shouldn't they also pay the associated taxes? When tabulating telephone bills, remember that in some cases, you're paying 15 percent of call charges in city, state, and federal taxes. Tabulate the cost according to each client's total and bill it out accordingly to that client.

Make the IRS your friend. Really. The kind folks at the Internal Revenue Service are friendly when it comes to giving out free information on how to run a home-based business within the guidelines of the tax code (or at least their interpretations of it). Log on to the IRS's Web site (www.irs. ustreas.gov) and look around for Publication 587, entitled *Business Use of Your Home . . .* or Publication 946, *How to Depreciate Property.* Learn what the IRS's feelings are on these particular issues. Summaries of IRS rules and regulations, educational downloads, and answers to frequently asked questions are also on the IRS's Web site.

Minimize confusion. Use one credit card for personal expenses, another for business. The IRS frowns on commingling of funds and accounts.

Separate your monies. Bank like a company, not like a household. Open a separate business bank account to isolate your business transactions. Shop around. Price shop. The banking climate is brisk and competitive. You may not get ATM access to business funds (some banks—and banking regulations, for that matter—won't allow it). But being an astute business customer may get you free checking or checks, free credit cards tied to the account, reduced-rate loans or lines of credit. It's called "relationship banking." And big institutional banks are coming to realize that small business customers are only growing in number and value.

Consider a credit union. When looking for a new bank, consider the credit union. Though most charge monthly service fees for business accounts, some credit unions pay interest on business checking accounts. You could get a form of "relationship banking" that traditional institutional banks only promise.

Get preclearance. If you have checks coming in regularly from particular clients that you know won't bounce, talk to your bank branch manager about getting them noted in the bank's computer system for immediate clearance. The bank usually will oblige. Then write "for immediate clearance" on the back of the check each time you make a deposit. It's your money. Get faster access to it.

Get that fee waived. Request that your bank card or credit card issuer waive the annual fee (often between $15 and $30); with so much competition around, banks are more interested in your business than the fee itself. For any credit card you use, make sure it comes with a standard extended product warranty product protection. That's less expensive than warranty options purchased with new equipment.

Bank online and by phone. Why wait until tomorrow to find out if a check or a deposit has cleared? Online banking and banking by telephone eliminate long times spent waiting for a live customer service rep at your monolithic institution. Besides, many banks are now charging customers every time they speak with a live operator regarding a matter that could have been answered electronically or via a Touch-Tone phone.

Print your own money. Got a business checking account? The last place to go for checks (even for your personal account) is the bank. It'll often get you for more than five times what a printing company would get for the same, if not more graphically attractive, checks—except, that is, when you're first opening the account. Hit up the customer service representative (CSR) for extra checks. To price checks, call Designer Checks (800-239-9222) or Current Checks (800-533-3973).

Make your checks as attractive as possible. Like other stationery and paper goods that leave your office, make your checks memorable. At least use some kind of statement on the check (possibly within the address box) stating what you do: "John Smith, Custom Commercial Photography." Or get your bank or check-printing company to open up its book of logos that can be printed on checks.

Fax after hours, and tally those tabs. Long-distance charges are lower and busy signals are fewer after hours. Also, faxes are there when the recipient comes to work in the morning. And remember to always bill for fax expenses.

Be an energy maven and kilowatt monitor. Have your power company perform a home energy survey; many will pay for upgraded insulation, higher efficiency air conditioners or furnaces, window treatments, or anything else that will lower your overall usage and make your home and office more comfortable during extreme weather. When you leave your home or home office, adjust the air conditioner (or use autoadjusting or timed thermostats) and turn off the lights; not only does this decrease energy use, turning off the lights also reduces heat. So too does turning off the computer when it won't be used for more than a few hours. A small utility fan blowing across the back of the computer will help cool the unit and the heat it otherwise would emit into the office.

Fax your literature. Create your brochure and sales, technical, or other literature on your computer and fax it—instead of mailing a printed version—when someone requests literature. The few minutes it takes to fax such a brochure will never add up to the cost of designing, preparing, printing, and mailing a brochure. And when faxing directly from the computer, images are sent much quicker than if they were being faxed through a dedicated fax machine.

Get covered. Insurance is not so difficult an issue for the home-based business as some would believe. Simply call your carrier and explain your setup. You might need a business rider to cover equipment related to the business and another to increase liability for customers, clients, or vendors who visit your home office. Your company and its vehicles should be rated correctly to ensure the best rate and maximum savings. By bringing auto and homeowners (and any other property or liability insurance you carry) to the same carrier, you might be awarded multiple policy discounts, which sometimes can slice 15 percent or more from some areas of coverage. Make sure you're not doubling up your coverage (carrying a rider on something the traditional homeowners policy covers). Repeat these steps each year, review your coverage, comparison shop, and don't be afraid to switch carriers if a better rate comes along.

Look to cop a job from Uncle Sam. The Small Business Administration sponsors Pro-Net, a procurement and marketing network service (PRO-Net.sba/gov). It's a search engine used by contracting officers for locating small businesses that can provide a needed product or service. It currently lists over 170,000 small, disadvantaged, and female-owned businesses. Get your business listed and registered on that database. Pro-Net is open to any small firm seeking federal, state, and private contracts. The database can be searched by business type, location, keywords, SIC codes, and more. The site also has links to other government procurement opportunities including the *Commerce Business Daily.*

RESOURCES

www.sbaonline.sba.gov

The Small Business Administration's SBA Online site includes plenty of small business info plus a sample business plan outline. It also is host to Small Business Administration Shareware, a library of 500 programs to support start-up businesses.

www.bbb.org

The Better Business Bureau Directory of Better Business Bureaus in the United States and Canada provides business alerts, information about dispute resolution, how to locate a branch bureau, and a resource library.

www.irs.ustreas.gov

The IRS home page takes a pretty fun feel for one of the nation's most feared government organizations. *The Digital Daily* is a colorful electronic publication that includes tax statistics, personal and business tax information and education, forms and publications, and a place to lodge your comments.

Organization
Files and Data Management Are the Glue That Holds Your Business Together

Files, files, files. If location is the rule of real estate, filing is the rule for small business. Your ability to access client information, past activity, and accounting data quickly and efficiently is key to your success. Just spend an hour unsuccessfully looking for a single document to know what this means. Some say more than a minute spent looking for *anything* in the office is a sign of a poorly organized office. While that may seem a little extreme, test yourself. Think of a document you haven't seen in a while, and hunt it down. How long did it take? Time for a filing makeover?

Create and use a good file system that reflects your specific needs. Files are your friends in the war against clutter and office mayhem. Become the envy of your industry peers by being able to access the finest minutia of data on a moment's notice.

Plan to grow. The first step in any filing program is to envision where the business will be three years or so down the road when your client list has grown. Will you have space to store the paperwork? Spend some time up front and you'll appreciate that time down the road. Buy the right filing cabinets and designate the right space to fit those cabinets.

Buy used cabinets. New filing cabinets can be expensive. Buy used and save money. If it's scuffed and marred, throw a quick coat of primer on it and paint it to match the office interior or place it out of sight in the closet, and it's as good as functional. Make sure your filing cabinets have full-extension drawers that provide access to rear files. Nothing's worse than having to remove files in front to access files in back.

Divide and conquer. Break large topics down into smaller categories for easier reference. Divide files into three categories for easier access and storage:

1. *Current:* client/customer files used daily or frequently that can be stored in a cabinet or in a file rack on the desktop or nearby shelves (preferably within arm's reach) for easier access.
2. *Recent:* papers downgraded from the current file but still needed close at hand (at least in the office filing cabinet).
3. *Archival:* files removed from recent use that can be stored in a box or unused filing cabinet.

Ditch, download, or destroy. Each month, visit *current* files and remove any documents that are either dated, no longer useful, or in need of refiling. Download to *recent* or ditch. Every six months, revisit each *recent* file and download to *archival* or ditch them to the trash. *Archival* files should be only those necessary for long-term client background or business information.

Bind 'em. Research information or other data you've collected over time on a particular subject can become an invaluable and recurring resource—only if it's accessible quickly. Put such data into a three-ring binder (one binder for each subject). Use tabbed dividers to further categorize the info. Then place it close at hand on your reference shelf (you *do* have a reference shelf for your dictionary, thesaurus, desk encyclopedia, and other reference materials?). This way, if a client or compatriot calls in a bind for some info, you can impress him or her with your expedient answer.

Index it. Create a computer file entitled "mktbindr" for the marketing binder, for example. Format a three-row column, then index the contents by article or data title, date, and tab category. Print it out and insert it into the cover. You'll be the model of efficiency.

Immediately sort all incoming data into "trash-it" and "keep-it" piles. Don't drown in a flood of incoming paper. Between mail, faxes, and even electronic mail, it's easy to let the sorting lapse and end up to your neck in pounds of paper. Tear and trash the "trash-it" pile right into the garbage. File the "keep-it" pile.

End each day by cleaning the desk. Shift papers into the "next phase" of your filing system. Leaving the day with a clean desk means you'll start tomorrow with a clean desk, and you'll appreciate that in the morning.

Don't let overpiled files get the best of you. Spend an hour every Friday plodding through files to sort them into their rightful places.

Shelve the clutter. What's a desk if it's layered in clutter? Hang shelves to get Rolodexes, current files, pen holders, personal knickknacks, and other everyday items off the desk. Without creating wall chaos that's visually annoying, put walls to use with hanging shelves, bookcases, or organizers that will lead to better control of the SOHO scene.

Use that space: Part I. Walls, desks, drawers, and nooks in the office closet are available for use. If there's a space not being used, there's a way to use it effectively. Stacking and hanging files can help capitalize on otherwise ill-used space. Hanging-file organizers use otherwise wasted wall space and create great "hot" job files that are used or referenced frequently. If there's a space on the desk that's not being used, stacking trays can "prioritize" that space. Ditto for the closet.

Use that space: Part II. The wall is a great empty space where you can use cork board to post important items and get them off the desk. Use a dry-eraser board to note and erase deadlines as they are scheduled and later met.

Tickle your memory bone. Ticklers are immediate gratification for those who want to stay organized. Ticklers can be as simple as writing notes in a date book or on the erasable wall calendar. Or get a small index-card box and a stack of cards, or an accordion folder with enough pockets for either each day of the month or each month of the year.

Then each morning (or night before, when preparing for the next day), scan the pocket for things to do. If you're into computer management, contact management software like ACT! can accomplish the same task. Even Windows 3.1 and Windows 95 software come with a simple calendar and scheduling application. Just drop it into the computer's "Start Up" menu so that the application opens automatically every time you boot the computer up.

Get your magazines under control. Periodicals piling up against you? Set aside time to read—or at least skim—each new publication that comes in the office. Important or pertinent articles should be flagged with a self-adhesive note on which the topic is written where it's visible from the outside. Then stack the articles chronologically. Every six months, pull some magazines from the bottom of the stack, browse through each to see if it's still relevant. If so, return it to the stack. If not, toss it into the recycling pile. If only one article is worth saving, tear it out and put it into the appropriate reference file.

Take it a page further. Ever come across a magazine or newspaper with a single article of interest? But you keep the publication around because you don't want to ditch the article? Tear and ditch. Pull the single article from the publication, toss the article into a "to read" file, and toss the publication into the recycling bin. Then toss that file into your briefcase or in-office hot file. Next time you have some time to kill, pull it out and give it a read. Then file the article in the appropriate office file.

Functional Efficiency

Analyze Your Work Style to Achieve Maximum Output

Take a look at the way you do business. Are you functionally efficient? Do you plan your day, week, month to capitalize on those things you need to do? Getting your home office ducks in a row will eliminate duplicated efforts. Focus on results, not keeping busy. This way you'll accomplish more projects.

Don't just do it—plan it. Start each morning with 15 minutes spent outlining the day's events. Make it part of your morning routine over coffee, juice, the paper, or the TV news. Then take it a step further by spending a half-hour every Sunday evening outlining the tasks or jobs to be completed or advanced over the coming week. But be flexible. Unexpected events or issues will arise that will need tending to.

Make lists. To-do lists. Call lists. Travel lists. All kinds of lists. Have self-adhesive note pads around the house; they're essential for taking down and posting quick reminders.

Call out. Spend the first 30 minutes of your day sending out a round of phone calls or completing items on your lists and watch the items get ticked off one by one.

Consolidate trips. Why drive excessively? When you're spending the day away from the office, schedule your day for efficient travel by grouping appointments geographically. Unless you know your clients' communities and streets as well as your own neighborhood, buy and use a street atlas.

Bank electronically and at night. Teller lines (OK, lines in general) are for wasteful boors and the time-impaired. Bank after hours by mail or a night drop box. Use an ATM to withdraw cash only. Many banks process overnight deposits on the next business day while processing ATM deposits in two days. Handle account inquiries and transfers by phone. And put that computer to better use. Bank online.

Create cheat sheets for frequently called numbers. Jotting down a short list of your most important numbers will save you from looking them up every day. Better yet, add them to your speed dial. Create cheat sheets for infrequently called numbers. Both will help you track elusive numbers—especially when billing clients for long-distance calls (you think you'll remember at the time you're dialing, but a month later you'll have forgotten, trust me).

Make your home and car conducive to capitalizing on spurts of inspiration. Brainstorm in the shower? Buy an erasable grease pencil and pad to hang on the wall. Brainstorm in the car? Keep a pad of paper and a handful of pens in the glove compartment. Carry a pocket-sized pad and pen. Scatter self-adhesive note pads around the house to jot down reminders and teasers for meetings and other information. Keep pads and pens near each telephone in the house.

Take notes. A reporter's notebook is a four-by-eight-inch spiral-bound pad that easily fits in the breast pocket of a jacket or in a back pants pocket and is usually sold in a bundle of 12. Devote one to each client so you'll have the client's notes or your thoughts in one place and handy for each meeting or project. Reporter's notebooks are not commonly found at the local office superstore, but the store will be happy to special order them.

Invest in a microcassette recorder. To record conversations, personal memos, and other important data, use a recorder and learn to speak freely into it (for some, it's not easy).

Download daily. All those notes sitting clumped on a desk or dictated into a recorder do nothing if not put into action. Take those notes and memos you've collected and download them daily to a single spiral pad, computer file, or another place where they'll get put into action.

Ship like a pro. Use mailing and shipping services like any corporation would—maybe even better. First, use a credit card to secure accounts with all the major shipping companies. Then, get their shipping software packages and packaging kits so you can create preprinted labels. Request packaging materials and then stash and recycle them. Use the companies' Web sites to schedule pickups, track packages, or determine shipping costs. But beware: Displayed shipping fees often are for account holders only and could be higher for nonaccount holders.

Branch out and go cheap. It's always more expensive to have an express package picked up than it is to leave it at a drop box. Using your zip code, locate the three to five closest drop boxes in every direction, radiating out like spokes on a wheel. That way, when you need to drop a package on your way somewhere, you can use the one that's on the way.

If overnight is a must, price shop. Why overnight it? Overnight service adds even more cost, so plan your shipping needs to avoid next-day delivery (and remember to check the appropriate box on the package).

Cop the overnight option. Even though shipping companies have a two-day option, most packages sent from and to a continental U.S. address will get there overnight. Just don't bank on it if it absolutely, positively has to get there overnight.

Weasel out your client's account number. When shipping to a client, feel out whether the client is open to your using its account number. If not, expense it out anyway (or at least factor it into your fee).

Buy an inexpensive postal scale. Postage is no guessing game. Never again overpay because you estimated postage (or got a package back marked "Insufficient Postage"). Log on to the U.S. Postal Service's Web site (www.usps.gov) and find out what its mailing rates and options are.

Copy at an office superstore. Consolidate your efforts when buying goods and making copies. Bundle your photocopy and office supply purchasing chores so you'll go to the superstore and open the wallet only once.

Get that package. Many shipping companies and couriers will not deliver to post office boxes, and many communities—especially gated neighborhoods—dissuade delivery of business packages to residential addresses. Use an executive suite or local storefront ship-and-receive service to receive packages or as your mailing address.

Each day, complete one more rote chore. From itemizing the telephone bill to preparing month-end billings or invoices, these tasks must be done. Completing them leads to a feeling of accomplishment. Better still, do them after hours. That way, you won't feel you've wasted daylight work time, and you'll feel good that you put in a little extra time on the business.

Each day, think of ten ways to improve your business. From operations to marketing, from sales to how you work at home, constantly strive to improve some facet of the operation. Your business is your baby, and it won't grow unless you nurture it passionately. The stronger your business gets, the more confident, proud, and strong you'll become. Find a business coach or manager whom you trust (maybe even a spouse, significant other, trusted family member, or close friend keen on business strategies) and evaluate your successes and setbacks at the end of every day, week, and month. Schedule a year-end/new-year planning session to be held away from the office to chart the past year's events and plot the coming year's course. Wear your thick skin and be as objective as possible. Plan to win.

SHIPPING SITES

www.usps.gov

The Web site of the U.S. Postal Service allows you to indicate a change of address, search out zip codes, calculate postage rates, or track Express Mail.

www.fedex.com

FedEx's site allows you to track packages, schedule pickups, locate the nearest drop box, figure out a shipping rate, and download free software.

www.ups.com

United Parcel Service's site also lets you track, calculate, locate drop boxes, and schedule pickups.

www.dhl.com

DHL Worldwide Express also lets you calculate, locate drop boxes, and schedule pickups as well as track in the United States and abroad and use international site locators; it even provides service bulletins on how shipments are running.

www.airborne.com

Airborne Express's site allows you to do everything its competitors' sites do plus even help you find a job in the company.

Communications
Phone, Fax, and E-Mail

Alexander Graham Bell couldn't have imagined . . . The phone is every business's lifeline to the world. To create a fully functional home office, the latest in telecom hardware can be the difference between optimum functionality and "just getting by."

Don't be "untouchable." In the communications age, there's no excuse for not being reachable—or at least letting clients know your plans. A voice mail, e-mail, fax, and/or telephone message each can help alert clients to your schedule, keeping them aware of when they can or cannot contact you.

Go wireless. When you're working solo from home, accessibility at all times during business hours (whatever you deem those hours to be) is essential. By investing in a good, two-line cordless telephone, you'll never miss a call when you're getting the paper or the mail, pulling weeds in the yard, or otherwise nowhere near a wired phone.

If you don't own a fax machine, find a nearby location that offers such a service. Find a fellow home-based worker in the neighborhood with whom you can share a fax machine and expenses.

Fax first. Ever print a document before you fax it to someone? Why not get a fax/modem and fax software? That way you'll save wear and tear on your printer, save paper and ink cartridges, and won't have to file an actual document when you're done. When faxing an actual paper document, use self-adhesive fax memos: they're shorter and cheaper than an entire cover page.

Make info easy to get. When leaving an outgoing message on your own machine, leave your e-mail address, fax number, and office address so callers can retrieve that information if needed. Also ask that callers let you know the best time to return their call.

Change your outgoing message frequently. Variety gets remembered. At least every week, change your message. Record a message that's an uplifting announcement spoken in a bouncy pleasant voice—both on your machine and on the machines of those you call. When recording your message, indicate your availability for the week, or day if appropriate. For example, if you're working on projects for clients who could be calling for updates, you might want to say, "You've reached John's office for the week of June 8. I'll be in the office all week"; or "I'll be out Monday and Tuesday mornings, returning in the afternoon, and I'll be in the rest of the week." Just don't make it too complicated.

Give them an out. If your voice mail provides callers an option to go straight to the beep, tell them up front on your outgoing message—especially if you're leaving all your contact information. Why make them muddle through a lengthy message if they've got an out?

Always leave your answering machine—and fax machine—on. Loathe it as we may, working from home provides clients greater access, and they will use and abuse it. But customer service is the mantra of the 1990s. So if a client calls after hours and you're not home, at least the machine will gather the message and details, and you can respond appropriately. Many people—even those who work in traditional offices—are taking work home with them, so when they get a spurt of inspiration at some odd hour, your answering machine (or fax machine) will answer their calls if you elect not to.

Access remotely. Make sure the answering machine you buy has remote access for retrieving messages and changing your outgoing message.

Know who's calling. Caller ID, which tells you who is calling, will help you filter out those calls the machine should get from those you must answer—especially after hours.

Learn telephone etiquette and style. Take notes on every conversation; sweating the details is essential to growing the business. Log every message on a spiral-bound notebook to have a record of who called when. Be genuinely courteous to your clients' assistants and secretaries (they're the gatekeepers to your target audience). And remember to keep all conversations—especially personal talks—brief and with one of two goals in mind: getting an assignment from an existing client or scheduling a meeting with a prospective client. You want nothing more than to hang up with a new assignment on the eraser board or a new entry in the date book.

Take the abuse. Clients will put you on interminable hold, toss you into voice mail jail, or hop off the line in a moment's notice when one of their clients come calling. And you'll smile. Their budgets are your income.

Never speak to clients over a speakerphone. Use the speaker function on your phone to dial numbers and pick up after the party has answered. Reserve the speaker function for calls where ease—not impressions—count (like directory assistance or dealing with nonclients or vendors).

Get vain. No matter how hokey, vanity telephone numbers, like 555-CORP, get remembered (remember the point of marketing?). They also show you cared enough to secure the number.

Go toll-free. An 800 telephone number is not just for Mega-Enormous Corp. any longer. For less than $10 a month plus a per-minute usage fee, home-based companies can give their customers and clients toll-free access for sales and information. While you're at it, secure a vanity number (800-productco), and match that with your traditional business line (212-productco) and your Web site (www.pro ductco.com). What's more, it looks really impressive on a business card to have an 800 or 888 number.

Make the phone company your buddy. From caller ID, answering services, and call forwarding to low-cost reliable answering services, investigate what they can do for you—you'll be blown away. Today's modern technology brings the functionality of the corporate office to the confines of the suburban home office and will help turn your home office into a streamlined, "transparent" operation.

Double your phone's capacity. Use call waiting to turn one line into two. Then use advanced caller ID, which requires you to purchase a call-viewing device, to find out who's calling while you're on the phone. Just remember: if your business phone shares a line with the fax machine, turn off call waiting before sending a fax (in most regions dial *70; it turns back on when you hang up).

Get a distinctive ring. Give your one-line office a second number that can be dedicated to a business line, a fax machine, or other business operation. The service's distinctive ring lets you know who (which business) or what (the fax machine) the caller is hoping to contact. By using a distinctive ringing line as a fax number, you can stop juggling phones when a fax tone is heard on the other line. By buying a Fax Switch, you'll have all incoming fax calls on the distinctive ringing function automatically transferred over to the fax machine.

Technology is your friend . . . know it . . . use it. Remember each product's feature, functions, and limitations. People spend extra money for all those gadgets and gizmos with their phones, cellular phones, fax machines, and answering systems. Then they don't put them to full use. Call waiting is useless if another phone in the home is off the hook. The speed dial function on a phone or fax is worthless if you don't program in some numbers. An answering machine that won't work with a fax machine to receive transmissions when you're out of the office is only doing half its job. Make your office fully functional by reading the instructions and applying your knowledge.

Consider automated voice messaging systems. If you don't like voice mail or are tired of losing messages to answering machines that died with the last power outage, go with an off-site service. Wildfire (800-WILDFIRe) is an application that can answer calls, forward them to off-site locations, and conference in programmed callers. Bogen MiniMail (Bogen 800-784-7493) can handle two telephone lines, forward calls to a cell phone or pager, notify you of a message, and has speed dialing and speakerphone capability. But as with any high-tech application, beware the functional learning curve. You don't want to lose calls while you're figuring out how to use all this new technology.

Shop around. Telephone companies are increasingly hungry for business. And they all want your home-based business. Investigate what different companies can do for you. Most have cost-saving billing plans and services and informative newsletters designed for the home office market. Use them; they're free!

Scrutinize each month's telephone bill. Check your own calling patterns, including time spent with individual clients or calls to directory assistance. Further, unless you're on a phone contract (and who is these days?) your long-distance company can change its rates with no warning.

Comparison shop your phone bill a few times a year. It's one of those recurring expenses that can be easily lowered.

Nickel and dime 'em. Nickel Sundays, ten-cent Mondays, free Fridays. Phone companies are practically giving their services away. Just consider for a moment a free Friday spent calling around the country pitching new work, not worrying about how long it takes to schmooze a new customer or build a relationship. Customers will think you care enough to spend a king's ransom talking with them. It'll cost you a fraction of that.

Pay up front. Some telephone companies provide an additional savings per minute for customers who agree to pay an approximate $5-a-month recurring charge. Some folks don't like paying up front. AT&T's One Rate Plus program will break even at around 100 minutes (given the 5¢-a-minute savings subtracted from the company's 15¢-a-minute One Rate plan). Those who switch from the standard pricing of 28¢ a minute to One Rate Plus will make up the up-front fee in little more than 21 minutes. If you're not billing back clients for telephone expenses, that's a lot of nickels.

Dial around. The new long-distance calling services that let anyone dial 1-0 and then a three-digit number require no commitment, contracts, or defection from your favorite provider. When you know you'll be on a long-distance call for a while (at least 20 minutes, which will result in a 50 percent saving on each such call, according to one provider), dial around. It will even show up on your regular monthly telephone bill.

Get served after hours. When interacting with your local or long-distance provider's customer service department, call after hours. Most are open 24 hours daily (or 24-by-7, as it's becoming known), and it will save time from calling at peak hours. Also, many of the services provided are automated so you can check on a payment or other account activity anytime.

Know the code. Many long-distance carriers offer features that assign billing codes or categories to each long-distance number called. These call management services categorize all toll calls, helping manage long distance calls and allowing customers to speed up the monthly process of attaching billable calls to client invoices. What's more, if you question whether a specific call was yours, you'll be more certain it was.

Consider next-generation modems. If you're thinking of adding business and fax lines and also need fast Internet access, then broadband, ADSL (asymmetric digital subscriber line), cable modems from your cable provider, and ISDN (integrated services digital network) provide a speedy connection to the Internet. Reasonably priced for the home office that needs fast connections to the World Wide Web, these digital data lines let users enjoy downloads at speeds once reserved for the corporate office. ADSL is increasingly available nationwide and provides fast Internet connections with nothing more than a new modem and software installed in the computer—all for about $40 a month. ISDN provides multiple telephone lines for faxing, talking, and logging on to the Internet and for sending or receiving e-mail all at once. In some markets, ISDN runs about $60 a month, plus an additional fee for the Internet service provider (ISP). Call your local telephone service provider to see if the service is available and then ask if your ISP can handle the faster connections. If not, most telephone companies providing the service also provide links to the Internet. For cable modem availability in your area, call your cable company.

Go cellular. Talk about staying in touch. The new digital personal communication services, or PCSs, and traditional cellular services available on the market today can turn every drive or trip to a client, even an outing with the family, into an extension of your office time. Pricing plans can give callers a prepaid "bucket" of hundreds or thousands of minutes for one flat fee. That's cheap airtime. One upshot: no contracts. One downside: many such "networks" are not national or global yet and have no "roaming" capabilities. Travel outside your "local calling zone" and the phone may become little more than an impressive dashboard ornamontht. Still, those zones are growing fast. And with often free caller ID and voice mailboxes, PCS phones can serve as a newfangled pager.

Get beeped. Like cellular pricing, pager pricing is no longer an excuse. It's just a matter of how many features you want. Stock quotes, latest headlines, sports scores, even the weather all are part of today's available pager products.

Be frugal with your expensive numbers. Decide if you want to leave your cellular number on your answering machine or printed on your business cards. It might get costly and unnecessarily abused if every client has access to your cellular number (beepers are a more likely choice to be given out freely). Some answering services or devices will automatically forward calls to your cell phone.

Appearances
Project the Right Image

Image is everything to some and nothing to others. Some home-based professionals strive to hide that they work from home. Others simply seek to maintain their professional image—while worrying little about clients' knowing they're home based. How you approach certain communications and image issues depends on which image you want to project to the world outside.

Take a title. You're no slouch. Why shouldn't your business card or corporate position say you are? Even if you run a small, one-person operation, take a position of power. Oft-used titles include president, chief executive officer, or chairman. Low-key? Then go for principal or partner. That certainly sounds better than "Humble Freelance Consultant."

Don't disappear. One essential "appearance" issue when working from home is to simply appear. No differently than teleworkers who spend so much time working from a home office that they fear "falling out of the loop" in the workplace, home-based workers must ensure they remain visible—at least in people's minds. Many home-based workers are so focused on producing their product or delivering their service that they become otherwise invisible to their clients, vendors, and industry peers. Sometimes it's difficult to get out and about. So make sure that in the course of daily affairs you maintain contact with your audience to let it know you're still around.

Be casually comfy—but aware of clients' perceptions. Is showered, shaved, and dressed for success your style? Or would you rather don shorts and a T-shirt? Comfort is king, but beware of clients who might drop by unannounced and see you casually dressed. Will that hurt their image of you— and your account with them?

Dress for success when heading out. How you look is the first and most important impression people will get of you—even if they've seen you before. If you're making a run to the local store during business hours, dress as if you'll be meeting a client. This is especially important if you carry sales information or a product sample everywhere you go. The logic is that because you've already determined you're prepared to make a sale on a moment's notice, you should look like a salesperson (but would *you* buy your product from you if you were dressed in torn jeans and a T-shirt?).

Be transparent. Use communications technology and the right mental strategy to maintain "transparency," or the appearance of being professional and not necessarily working from a home office. Consider whether a poor mental impression from an aging answering machine with a faded outgoing message would hurt your clients' perceptions of you as a vendor. If done right, the home office can appear like any downtown tower—or at least not like a home office.

Make sure your answering machine or service sounds professional. Machines that sound like answering machines break down any semblance of the corporate setting (if that's what you're striving to achieve). Answering services also often provide greater functionality and feature-laden technology than a simple machine (like taking calls when the phone is in use or allowing easy remote retrieval of calls).

Create a message that leaves the right impression. "You have reached the office of John Smith. I'm either on the phone or away from my desk right now. Please leave a message, and I will call you back." If one telephone line serves both home and home office, tell clients who may call after hours, "Call me after hours, I'm working late tonight" or "All calls are forwarded to my home after hours."

Hire a "voice" for your outgoing message. Find someone with an attractive or dignified voice (a Brit or other foreigner with a unique accent could sound cool), write some copy, and have the "someone" read your message. At the very least, you'll provide food for thought for incoming callers. And they'll think you run a large(r) operation.

Never leave them hanging. If you're leaving for a few days, record a message on your voice mail saying you'll be away and whether you'll be checking messages. Tell people whether to expect a return call. Also, call your clients for whom you're currently working on an assignment and let them know you'll be away. It's also a good idea to tell clients for whom you've recently delivered a project that you'll be traveling, so if they have any questions or need immediate attention, the onus will be on them to contact you sooner— or later.

Take on a few "virtual" employees. When another person in the home office—spouse, employee, teenage child—answers the phone properly, it gives the impression that the operation has more than a sole proprietor at the helm. Ensure that the speaker's tone, demeanor, and words are professional, even having a few trial runs to make certain the speaker will convince any client.

Farm out your messages. An answering service to which all calls can be forwarded after hours or when you're out on an appointment also gives a professional impression. Screen the services first to ensure you find their demeanor appealing. Then spot check. Call occasionally to see how many rings it takes for your service to answer. Call late in the evening or early in the morning to see what the service sounds like off-peak. You want to make sure the voices answering your phone are voices you'd want to hear answering your phone.

Make your space official. When writing your address or ordering a rubber stamp for putting your return address on letters and other correspondence, call "Apt. B-104," for example, "Suite B-104" or "No. B-104." It appears more officelike than a residential address.

Leave that confining home-based space behind. An executive suite can be an ideal place to hold a conference or meeting in a room that's significantly larger than your dining room. Rent a suite by the hour or negotiate a better rate for a week or longer.

Go "virtual" when traveling. When traveling and visiting clients on the road, an executive suite can be a perfect place to hold a meeting. Use the services of a national chain like Atlanta-based EBC Office Centers, San Francisco-based

HQ Network Systems, or even Office Depot, which operates Images small business centers featuring copy services and workspace, or Kinko's, which offers "virtual office" space for telecommuters, home-based workers, and "road warrior" sales staff. Not only is an executive suite suitable for daily work and meetings, but the variety of services—from receiving mail and calls to sending faxes and providing efficient work space when the home office is unavailable—can increase efficiency and productivity. Call the Executive Suite Association in Columbus, Ohio, at 800-237-4741 to learn more, and to receive a list of member facilities to keep in your briefcase.

Sleep easy at business-equipped hotels. Plan out-of-town stays at hotels with small conference or meeting facilities and modern audiovisual equipment. Get chummy with a good business travel agent, who can then make recommendations on quality business-oriented hotels in your destination city. Or do your own research to find one or two hotel chains that offer such amenities as 24-hour business centers, room phones with data ports for plugging in the laptop, or even in-room faxes. Then get the directory of all the chains' locations. As with an airline or rental car company, by building a rapport with the right hotelier, you might be privy to some perks (like free meeting space or discounted service or refreshments) that will help your efforts appear seamless. It might help you woo and win over your client—or potential client.

Choose high numbers. When opening a new business account, have the bank customer service representative start the check numbers at 2,350, or another high figure. Some companies see low number checks and get antsy about dealing with start-ups. Banks usually don't care where the sequence starts, and it will make you look like you've been in business longer than you may have been.

Connecting

Compute to Empower Your Home Office

Technology is your friend, and information will be the currency of the 21st century. Become a purveyor of data, or at least be able to access and transmit. Logging onto computer and high technology levels the playing field and keeps all businesses in touch with the world's data flow. With powerful computers priced below $2,000 and telephone technology wiring the world, this is no time to be fearful of the PC. The world is becoming increasingly wired. If you're not plugged in, you'll be unplugged.

Don't make price an issue. The price of computer technology is dropping about as quickly as the creation and use of payment plans are growing. So there's no reason that a company that needs even a powerful computer should be without. Between local retailers offering 12 months-same-as-cash terms and national direct marketers and catalog companies devising newfangled, low-rate payment options, booting up and logging on is cheaper than ever.

Call on Uncle Sam. While the cost of new computer equipment can still be daunting to the average small business, most business equipment purchases are tax deductible up to a certain level. So whatever your concerns about the cost of computer equipment, let the government help you out. Consult your tax adviser on how to handle such issues.

Be an informed consumer. What will you need? Talk to your peers or read your trade journals to learn about some of the best hardware—and especially software—for your profession. Some might make do with off-the-shelf ensembles that include a word processor, spread sheet, and database. Other companies might need to complement those applications with industry-specific software for accounting, law, or desktop publishing. These can be expensive. So read up before doling out.

Log onto professional use groups. By accessing these sites in your profession, you'll get some insight and develop camaraderie with industry peers. Visit shareware sites (like www.shareware.com) to download and sample valuable—and often free—software applications.

Enroll in an adult education course. Been to high school lately? To learn the how-tos of new software and computer applications by signing up for inexpensive classes offered at a local high school or community college. Typically, the courses run in sequences, so once you've mastered the entry-level course on one piece of software, for example, you can move to a course on more advanced features.

Communicate electronically. Find out if your clients use e-mail via the Internet, and log on. In the Information

Age, businesses will communicate electronically. It's an efficient, almost immediate, and cost-effective way to stay in
touch. Once relationships are established by telephone,
many companies "speak" almost exclusively via e-mail. After
all, it's cheap, easy, fully documentable, and kind of fun.
Once you get the hang of it, you'll start sending and receiving
jokes to and from compatriots.

E-mail, e-mail, e-mail. When possible and appropriate,
send information, transcripts, reports, or other correspondence via e-mail or as e-mail attachments. It saves paper
and allows the recipient to edit or alter the text electronically. But assume nothing before hitting "enter." Inquire
what software the recipient has before sending a message—
otherwise he or she might not be able to open the file. A safe
bet is to save and transmit text files as ASCII attachments,
which can be opened by even older versions of software.

Back up, power up. *Always* back up data from your
hard-drive to a floppy disk, ZipDrive, JazDrive, or tape. Losing data is a bear. And buy and use an uninterrupted power
supply (UPS). Losing data to power outages is frustrating
beyond compare! Finally, hook that UPS into a surge protec-
tor (assuming there isn't a surge-protecting fuse plugged
into the back of the computer already).

**Shut down and unplug the computer during electrical
storms.**

Make the Internet your friend. When making any purchase—from a computer to insurance and appliances or
equipment for your business—use the Internet to conduct a
global information search. Many vendors have Web sites

containing product, pricing, and ordering information. This can be a tremendous time saver. Also, your research may lead you to a less expensive alternative.

Use your electronic library to access the world. Need some research for an upcoming project? Log on and learn more. Many universities, organizations, business associations, and trade publications have a Web site. Finding the site you want sometimes is just a matter of typing www.xyzproduct.com and seeing what pops up. And use search engines. They're like a card catalog (remember those?) and librarian all in one but are more inclusive than the former and talk less than the latter.

Make the Internet your industry library too. No doubt the publications you find useful have a presence on the World Wide Web (or if they don't, they will soon). Search out those titles useful to you, bookmark them, and start your day by visiting them.

Use the Internet to learn more about your industry. Create a profile of your market segment, study your niche's demographics, learn more about the people and companies you serve. Spot economic trends before they happen, then propose changes to your clients. They'll be impressed. They'll be awed. And it's hoped they'll be inspired to send you a contract for business.

Browse and bookmark. Spend some time browsing the Web to find your own resources; then create a "bookmark" for your personal favorites. These can include info on running a profitable home-based business or any resource you might find useful.

Become a news junkie. Start each workday with a search of the resources that show what's happened in your industry. Internet "Push" technologies will ferret out news stories or press releases you might find interesting and bring them to your mailbox.

Subscribe to use groups pertinent to your area of interest. Use the Internet to search for lists or online "clubs" of people interested in the same thing. Grouped by category, these services let participants float ideas, pick brains, learn more, and implement what they've learned. (See "Web Resources" below for ways to access the list that's right for you.)

Never lose that personal touch. Computers provide effective, nearly immediate communications. But never forget the personal touch of a phone call or a letter. You can't shake hands with a bit or a byte.

Get a Web site. No Web site? Are you kidding? With prices falling in both Web site design software and hosting space, the arguments for *not* having a personal Web site are quickly being exhausted. Besides, you'll never drop a dime on postage sending promotional kits to new business prospects. Just say, "Visit my Web site at www.product.com" and imagine their eyebrows rising—especially if they know you work from home.

Partner with an ISP. If the Internet is the "great equalizer" for business, then it also is for Internet Service Providers. This is not a business of "bigger is better." Quality site design and Web-site hosting can be found inexpensively from small ISPs—who are as hungry for work and as dedicated to deliver as you are.

Take Web site design in-house. Craft your own professional Web page with any of the off-the-shelf software available on the market. All you'll need once it's done is a host (that's *not* something the SOHO entrepreneur wants to do in-house).

WEB RESOURCES

Use these resources to learn more or to delve more deeply into the Internet . . .

www.thelist.com

The List provides a comprehensive directory of thousands of Internet Service Providers (ISPs) or the companies that businesses use to gain access to the Internet. Searches can be performed by state or area code and include individual company services, fees and rates, and contact information.

internic.net

InterNIC is the registration clearing house for domain names, or the part of a URL that falls between the www. and the .com or .net. Registration costs $70 for the first two years and $35 each year thereafter.

Motivation
Keep It Going

Competitors pop up out of nowhere. Repeat clients run thin. The marketing plan seems stuck on a plateau, and every cold call you place to follow up a mailing or solicitation is met with cold rejection. Essentially, the honeymoon has ended, and a comfy—if confining—job back at the corporate hive is looking all the more enticing. No expenses, no self-employment taxes, no health insurance premiums to worry about. Just a paycheck that comes like clockwork.

Almost every business experiences a honeymoon period. For the typical home-based enterprise, that ebbs after about 18 months. What you do next could determine whether the business succeeds or fails. Concentrate on bringing in new business, expanding existing client billings, building relationships that will help the enterprise solidify its market position. Plan for anniversaries. Plan to be here tomorrow.

Minimize distractions. Talk to any home-based worker or industry pundits and they'll bark out tales of woe about the distractions that abound in the home office. The fridge, dogs who need walking, weeds that need pulling, a house that needs cleaning. Then they warn about the bad tidings that befall the worker who succumbs to the allure of the home chore. Hogwash. Set your own flexible work style for this flexible work environment, and adjust it as necessary. If you've got a yen for cleaning the floors *now* and your work load's light, then do the floors. You'll probably be less focused if it's bothering you all day anyway.

Divert the diversions. Working alone is like being alone in a vacuum with nothing but the fridge, the yard, Jerry, Oprah, Regis, and Kathie Lee as your loyal friends. Problem is, none of them pay the bills or add much to the revenue stream. So getting and staying motivated is important to being successful and staying on top of your game.

Become a cheerleader. Motivation starts from within. As with any business, every day spent working from home won't be Christmas. Success and failure will come hand in hand. If only for your own psyche, learn to be upbeat—from the message you leave on your voice mail to the way you answer the telephone and conduct your daily affairs. A good attitude and positive outlook can be infectious; spread the positive vibes.

Don't let paranoia destroy you. Occasional failure can get the solo flyer to thinking . . . "Am I losing my edge? Are my clients leaving me? Is this a harbinger of things to come?" Flush such thoughts out of your head. In a small business, every day won't be an unmitigated success. Sometimes you win, sometimes you come up short.

Work hard to build receivables. When just starting out, countless things will stress you out, not the least of which is that lost revenue stream of the former day job. Receivables are a necessary evil that eventually (and you hope) morphs into cash—the business's life blood. Once the billings rise, checks will start flowing and it'll almost be like an annuity that comes in—just on an irregular schedule. You'll never have anticipated the postman so much.

Don't procrastinate. Learn how to conquer procrastination. Learn and exercise discipline. List your most urgent projects or tasks. Focus on one. Finish it. Move to the next. Undisciplined scatterbrains accomplish little.

Keep the date book filled. Nothing kills motivation more than idle time. Besides, a filled date book keeps you out, networking with business associates and potential clients or customers.

Don't get dogged by the naysayers and pessimists. Negative vibes can damage the spirit. So put up a force field to protect yourself from them. If someone doubts what you do (and they will at first), use that as motivation. Prove them wrong by succeeding.

Keep bridges strong and fortify weak ones. As a solo flyer, you'll also have to deal with animosity and jealousy from some workers in the corporate tower. While some are seeing the benefits of teleworking and working from home, many—especially midlevel managers—still resent that they're stuck with a commute to a downtown office and you're playfully hanging out in a home office, munching ice cream and playing with the kids in the yard. You can just imagine a wink of their eye and the chuckle in their voice when they speak of your "work" arrangement. Convince them that you're working. Tell them to judge you by the quality of your work, not the office from which—or the hours during which—it's created.

Take lunch over the news or newspaper. Keep light reading around as stimulating brain food. Always be consuming information. When the batteries run low or the imagination's ragged, have a few quick-play games in the PC to unwind—but don't become a video game junkie.

Avoid isolation. One of the biggest complaints from home-based workers is the isolation that comes from working alone. Network with others in your industry to keep connected to the world outside. This will also help stimulate the right brain by keeping pertinent conversation flowing.

Combat becoming a recluse. Create an advisory board of friends, family, or others in similar—but not necessarily competitive—businesses to keep ideas flowing and personal relations current. Maybe include local professors for whom you've spoken or provided input for their classes. Schedule group meetings or networking sessions, not to build business, but to spur creative thinking. Hit a retreat, the beach, the mountains. Pack a picnic meal, breathe the fresh air, and brainstorm today's life and tomorrow's business plan.

Health

Preserve Your Mind and Body

Working from home can reinvigorate a worker's health, mind, and body, or it can drain it. How you treat your home-based business will determine how you're affected by the sometimes subtle, sometimes blatant, demands of the workplace. Good health is a fusion of forces that work together to energize the body and spirit. Best part is, most of us learned them as youngsters—though we might not have continued using them along the way.

Eat right. Want to lunch on that plate of leftover pasta from last night? Well, do you have time for an afternoon nap? Snacking on fruits, vegetables, and light meals during the day can keep your body from becoming fatigued and can keep creativity flowing.

Exercise. It invigorates the body and soul and if implemented as part of a daily routine can be a healthy way to start or end the day. When in a creative rut or tired around midafternoon, take a walk, swim, bike, or go to the gym. No shower required when you're returning to the solitude of the home office. What's more, walking, riding a bike or stationary cycle, or even mowing the yard or working outdoors can foster introspection that can be used to rethink a perplexing work issue or otherwise clear the mind.

Sleep well: Part I. Whatever you need for a good night's sleep—eight hours or five—make certain you get it regularly. There will be crunch times that lead to less sleep. But average your sleep patterns out over the week and make sure you get what you need. Poor sleep habits creep up on you and after a few days you're dog tired.

Sleep well: Part II. Power down to power up. Getting woozy around midafternoon? Take a 20-minute power nap and awake a new person. No worries about what the former boss would say if he or she caught you with your head laid on the desk trying to energize for the afternoon work crunch. At your home office, your bed removes any burden of an uncomfortable siesta. It also removes the stigma. Twenty minutes of shut-eye and you'll awake refreshed and recharged. And if you have a bedside business phone, you won't miss a beat—just remember to pause a few seconds before answering and speak a few words before talking to the caller. We mustn't sound like we were caught napping.

Sleep well: Part III. If health insurance is a requirement of modern life, then get it as inexpensively as possible. Many solo flyers rely on a spouse's benefits coverage to ensure they're taken care of. But when it's time to shop for health insurance, there's power in numbers. When pricing insurance, shop around. Hit the Better Business Bureau, the local chamber of commerce, the local or national home-based business association. Many organizations offer group policies that are less expensive than those offered individuals.

But beware: sometimes they're not less expensive. Just because a group policy comes along doesn't mean it's cheaper than one you found on your own.

Go ergo. Ergonomics is not just for the big office. Ergonomics, or the science of fitting the worker to the workspace, has a place in every office—home and otherwise. Still cradling a phone between your shoulder and ear? Do your feet dangle just above the floor when you're sitting in your office chair? Is your view of the computer sort of off-kilter? Not good.

Analyze your angles. Ergonomics boils down to playing the angles. Is your chair supporting you in the right places and at the right height so your elbows form right angles and your hands are perched gently above the keyboard with no oft-used item on the desk (the mouse, the phone, or constantly retrieved tools like pens or paper) more than a quick, 15-to-30-inch reach away? Is your view of the monitor (which itself should be between 18 and 24 inches from your nose) at a slightly downward tilt from the horizon? Do your feet lay flat on the ground, or if not, are they propped on a telephone book or a foot rest (with funky little rubber massage nodules protruding into and gently massaging your soles)? Yes? Good.

Ditch that pain in the neck. Consider a telephone operator's headset (less than $100 at any large office retailer). Light and easy to use, your neck, ear, back, and body will be grateful. Better yet, get mobile. Use a cordless headset. Then you'll be free to wander while working.

Give your wrists a rest. A computer keyboard rest will help maintain correct wrist alignment and reduce pressure on your wrists. An ergonomic mouse pad will help alleviate awkward angles and pressure on your hands and wrists (a left-handed user should use a left-handed mouse). And when not typing or using the mouse, relax with your hands off the accessories.

Give your eyes a break. Frequently look away from the desk or monitor, focus on a distant object, and blink to moisten your eyes.

Use a document holder. When doing straight typing, position your documents on a document holder that is roughly the same distance and height as the computer monitor. This will help eliminate neck pains from viewing papers laid flat on the desk and eye strain from having to refocus for different distances.

Take a break. Sitting at the computer for hours on end is not what the human frame was designed for—and no chiropractor or human factor engineer (or "ergonomist") can remedy that. Take a break every 30 minutes.

Implement a scheduled stretch regimen. Use software that reminds you to take breaks during the day. Stretch your arms, wrists, hands, legs, and feet to attain a full range of motion. Clasp your fingers, turn your palms away from your body, and stretch the muscles of your arms. Clasp your hands behind your lower back and pull your shoulders back. Rotate your neck, chin to chest, ears to shoulders, eyes peering skyward. Or take a walk around the office. The point is to move that body.

Readjust your seating and keyboard every time you sit back down. And remember to change your seated position and stretch frequently during the workday.

Breathe easily. Replace air filters frequently to keep dust and allergens under control. Clean the monitor regularly with a glass cleaner to remove dust that could impair or dull your view of the screen. Keep your work surface, keyboard, and mouse clean of dust and particulates that cause allergies and eye strain. Dirty mice function poorly and can malfunction. Less dust is good on the sinuses, lungs, and overall health. And cleanliness *looks* better too.

Don't become a workaholic. Did your corporate boss ever tell you not to overwork? In the home office, it's a very real problem. Not only does overworking consume one's private life, it can stifle all the other things that would otherwise promote a healthy mind and body—like eating well and exercising regularly. Realize that overworking can take over your life—before it happens. Set limits on your workday (except maybe in times of a deadline crunch) and adhere to them.

Think safe, be safe. Personal safety is one of the most overlooked issues of working from home. When prospective clients stop by, who knows their intent? Schedule initial meetings at a neutral off-site location to give you time to get a feel for their character. If you never quite get the right vibe, but don't necessarily feel threatened, just say your office is no place for a meeting and meet at an executive suite location or local restaurant during nonrush hours.

Get PO'd. Your business card is no place for your home address—even if it *is* where you work. At about $20 every six months, a post office box is an ideal business address to put on literature. One consideration: many shipping services don't deliver to PO boxes. So consider a local pack-and-ship storefront or an executive suite as an address to place on your stationery. For a small fee, a storefront or suite will gladly sign for your deliveries and keep them until you arrive.

Get alarmed. Not a bad idea to install an alarm system, possibly with a panic button or keypad in your home office itself. If the room is full of expensive equipment, it might be worth the investment to prevent a theft.

Stick it to 'em. Plant thorny bushes outside every window around your home, especially outside your office. Landscaping not only adds to the value and appearance of your home, but Spanish bayonets, cactus, bougainvillea, and other thorny plants will make access prickly. And as they grow, they'll obscure the view in from outside (while providing those inside a typically better view out).

Prepare the office for travel. When traveling for a few days or longer, back up important data files and hide those diskettes somewhere safe. Then treat your home office like your home. Turn on a few lights, put others on automatic timers. Lock all the windows and doors to the outside, and lock the door from the office to the house. Turn off the automatic garage door opener. Set the alarm. Then go.

Make it safe. From the curb to your office itself, is your home office a safe place to work or visit? Are there paver bricks or stepping stones sticking up that may cause someone to trip and fall (a mantra in the personal injury law business)? Is your dog aggressive? Should it be closed in a bedroom when customers arrive? Talk it over with your homeowners insurance agent to ensure you have sufficient liability coverage.

Zen and the Home Office
Life Is a Ball Game; Play to Win

If life is in fact a ball game, as shoe and beverage companies would like us to believe, you must not only play to win. You must also learn to hit curve balls. Not every pitch will be down the middle of the strike zone. A lucrative client's call for an urgent project on yesterday's deadline—not an altogether uncommon demand—sometimes will come while you already are working on yesterday's deadline for another client. How you react speaks volumes about your character and your ability to play in the big leagues. Stress management will help relieve angst from your day and add happiness to your life.

Think outside the lines. The lines—or conventional wisdom—are *not* your friends. They are confining little queues designed to keep those within them from venturing beyond. Scribble, doodle, scratch, and scrawl outside the box. Traditional thinking is for traditional businesses. Home-based entrepreneurs are nothing if not nontraditional. Hit the library or local bookstore and browse through some of the magazines and books on the latest business trends. Call your mentor at the SBA, SCORE, or the county extension service (remember him or her from "Tools"?) and ask for guidance in promoting creative thinking. Brainstorm with fellow business owners to promote bursts of inspiration and let the free thinking flow.

Reinvent the wheel. Constantly reinvent and retool your company and your professional skill sets to adapt to ever-changing market conditions. This will create career stability in an unstable business climate. Become an industry futurist by reading industry journals or pertinent periodicals to learn of the shifts in your specialty area. If your industry or market segment takes a turn to the right, be well read enough to anticipate it months in advance. Make that turn before anyone else does, then sell yourself as the consultant who'll help others turn early as well. In an evolving business environment, you too must evolve—or perish.

Diversify. Nothing can kill a business more quickly than losing the one client who makes up the majority of the revenue stream. If you have one solid client, that's great. Strive to add another, then another, then another—never sacrificing service to an existing customer to expand the business. Which leads to another point: since home-based businesses typically have one employee—usually the sole proprietor—always realize when you and the business are being spread thin. Be prepared to turn down work so as not to sacrifice quality. Your name, product, and service level are your bond, and you are only as good as your last delivered project.

Be an opportunist. Working from home and being your own boss means opportunity knocks at different hours and with different offers. Are you ready to answer? If you're fixed on one professional mind-set, you might not be prepared to capitalize on chances that come your way, especially those you weren't prepared to master. Get out from within those lines. Be agile. Think differently. Change your business mindset.

Become an explorer. Think of life and business as an expedition. Unlike your office-based counterparts, as a home-based worker you get an opportunity to explore yourself and your relationships. You can capitalize on free time and find your personal and circadian rhythm. Take a day off to explore opportunities or whims—without logging a mental health day on some corporate time sheet.

Relax. Take breaks. Don't become a guilt-ridden, workaholic, work-at-home junkie. If you were a nine-to-fiver, you'd occasionally try to slip out for some free time. Now, you're the boss. Take advantage of the title. Cut yourself some slack.

Always reward yourself for a job well done. No matter how small or large the success, when you complete a significant assignment, win a new account you've been seeking, reach a sales milestone, or celebrate a business anniversary, recognize your success and celebrate the moment. Being home based means being cheerleader as much as wage earner. Buy yourself a trinket for the office or a new piece of software you've been wanting. Take the family out to dinner (after all, they are part of the office support staff). Or take some compatriots, advisory board members, or networking group partners out for a round of drinks (then the outing likely would be tax deductible). Jobs done well should be rewarded.

Make the home office homelike. *Home office,* after all, begins with home. Unlike the cubicle at the downtown office tower, the home office should say who you are. Hanging personal items around a workspace is an excellent way to keep the brain inspired. Make the office warm, inviting, and personal. Enliven it with pictures, posters, family photos, mementos, and knickknacks that brighten the office. Tape some of the kids' drawings to your wall or shelves right next to your occupational license. As long as the office doesn't lose its functionality, then go wild with the visual stimulation.

Keep playful fidget toys around. A rubbing stone, a hockey puck, or a baseball, for example, can provide tactile stimuli and spur creativity.

Bring plants into the office. They add life, help clean the air, and create a more biofriendly atmosphere. If the office has a window to the world outside, plant foliage outside the office window. Hang a bird feeder in a tree just outside the office window to attract life.

Bring a pet to work. From a hamster to a reptile or fish, small pets in the office add life and diversion when creativity has waned. Remember, though, that a soft, furry rodent likely will draw affection from the family—even when you're working.

Become part of the world outside. If your workload or your head can handle it, move outdoors. Brew some iced tea, grab the portable phone, break out some paperwork, put the PC on a wheeled computer desk—or take out the laptop—and hit the patio. Enjoy the environs and fresh air. Move your imagination. This isn't for those days that require hard-core concentration and no daydreaming. It's for when work can be done beyond the four-walled confines of the office.

Enliven your ears. How about audio stimuli? Music played quietly on a small stereo or your PC's CD-ROM drive with multimedia kit provides background sounds to stir the mind. Your favorite classical or even rock CD can do wonders to get the adrenaline flowing. While it's often best to go with vocal-less selections, you'll come to find that the words become just another instrument in the background—heard but not necessarily listened to.

Read, listen, and learn. Education doesn't end with school, and other people's stories of success and failure can be invaluable lessons. You will always be a student. It's just that the yearning for education now must be found within.

Do the best you can, but avoid the trappings of perfection. Giving 110 percent is different from being perfect all the time. Allow yourself some mistakes, but learn from them—and don't repeat them.

Foster the input and feedback from your clients. Creative and critical advice can be a rarity in the home office. It's important to make sure your work is what your clients expect. They may not tell you without your asking them. So ask. Better yet, send out a questionnaire once or twice a year soliciting their input. Beg them to be honest. Offer yourself for a face-to-face discussion on your performance—not quite a job evaluation and certainly not a kiss-up session where you're hoping to make clients feel good by giving them an audience. Ask for honesty; they'll appreciate the offer, and the gesture might take the professional relationship to a higher, warmer level.

Ask, then listen . . . carefully. If your clients offer feedback on your ideas, proposals, or work, take to heart what they're saying. This isn't lip service. And just because you've done the same project for them before, don't take lightly their instructions this time around. Overlooking the slightest change in a work order could spell disaster for the client relationship. In today's business climate, customer service is king. And that includes recognizing and putting into action clients' outright or subtle suggestions, requests, and ideas.

End each day by catching your breath. Consider your successes and figure out how to duplicate them tomorrow. Consider the day's hurdles not cleared, and figure out how to jump higher the next day. Then sit back and plan for the next day.

Be uplifting. Don't reflect the drudgery of everyday life. Smile and dial. Every time you speak to someone—especially potential clients on the telephone—be bright, energetic, inspirational. Leave them thinking of you as a charming, warm, and uplifting person to talk to—and work with! And don't just act. Make it your way of being.

Get inspired. Find a copy of the Desiderata—or a narrative, a verse, or a picture equally inspirational—and hang it in your office. The Desiderata is a great nonsectarian devotional to begin each day with. "Go placidly amid the noise and haste and remember what peace there may be in silence . . ."

Think and dream success. Imagine yourself more successful tomorrow than you are today. Spend 30 minutes every night imagining success. Imagine yourself meeting a big deadline, shaking your client's hand with that satisfied smile on both your faces, receiving that check in the mail. Imagine what it will take to get there, then make it so.

Chart an inner path. Personal and professional stagnation yields nothing but bad vibes. So where do you want to go in your life? What are your personal and professional goals? Write them down—all of them, whether there are 8 or 80 on the list. Then spend some time looking them over. You want to begin each day with some exercise? Write a business book or article, teach a class or speak on your topic to build your business, travel more, learn to play an instrument, do a weekend event with the family? Choose one, focus all your attention on it, and challenge yourself to achieve that goal within the next few months.

Eschew complacency and pump adrenaline. Too many businesses strive for short-term goals, only to become complacent once they've been achieved. And once in that rut, it's difficult to dig your way out. Determine what your peak capacity is and then add 110 percent of your mental energy. Always strive to achieve more—for yourself, for your family, for your future. Break out of the grips of complacency and comfort. Take your morning walk a different route each day. Drive or walk the kids to school a different way. Break up the status quo in your personal life, and it may subtly shift the course of your business life as well. Ruts become all encompassing and engulf your energy and spirit. Experiment. Reenergize yourself. A little adrenaline caused by the anxiety and stress of not having done something before can be exhilarating. You'll feel sharper, more creative, on your toes, and ready to take on the world. Feel the confidence. Isn't it powerful?

Strive for complete, utter, and unmitigated happiness. Settle for nothing less than what you want. You're already working from home, so you're halfway there. Now, succeed in business, and close the deal.

Index

About the Author

Jeffery D. Zbar is a journalist, author, and speaker in the small office/home office (SOHO) and teleworking fields. Married with three young children, he has spent much of the past decade developing a successful independent writing business from his home office in south Florida. He writes a regular column on advertising and is a feature writer on home office issues for the Fort Lauderdale *Sun-Sentinel*, and he contributes articles on business and alternative work styles to national publications. He is also a frequent speaker on marketing and workplace issues, and a coleader for CompuServe's Work-at-Home with Kids Forum. Client publications include *Advertising Age, Computerworld, Florida Trend, Home Office Computing,* and *Small Business Computing & Communications* magazines. Visit his Web site at www.goinsoho.com.